Backroad and Offroad Biking

JULES OLDER

STACKPOLE
BOOKS

0   11557 03150   8

Published by
STACKPOLE BOOKS
5067 Ritter Road
Mechanicsburg, PA 17055
www.stackpolebooks.com

Printed in China

10 9 8 7 6 5 4 3 2 1

First edition

Cover design by Wendy Reynolds
All photos by Effin Older

Library of Congress Cataloging-in-Publication Data
Older, Jules
      Backroad and offroad biking / Jules Older.
          p.   cm.
      Includes bibliographic references.
      ISBN 0-8117-3150-2 (paperback)
      1. All terrain cycling. I. Title.
GV1056.O43 2000
796.6'3—dc21
                                                                    00-025640

CONTENTS

1 The Joys of Backroad and Offroad Biking 1

2 Buying and Fitting the Right Bike 5

3 Accessories, Gear, and Clothing.............................. 35

4 Riding Paved Roads... 47

5 Riding Dirt Roads.. 57

6 Riding Offroad 65

7 Family Biking 91

8 Extending the Biking Season 103

9 Bike Care..109

10 Rider Care..137

11 Competitions, Races, and Schools 153

Resources 161

DEDICATION

To Effin Older, ace photographer,
who has ridden with me every inch of the way.

A mountain of thanks to those who have made this book all it could be. They are, in alphabetical order, Sunny Blende, Jean-Marc Blais, Melissa Bray, Kate Carter, Greg Danford, Andrew Herrick, Ben Hewitt, Paul Kennett, David Nesbitt, Steve Occleshaw, Effin Older, Ned Overend, Greg Padley, David Porter, Larry Reed, The Romp Family, John Schubert, Randy Swart, Phil Sweet, Jesse Terhune, Willie Weir, and Lennard Zinn. My thanks to all.

Extra special thanks to two of them, Effin Older and David Porter. Effin is not only the book's intrepid photographer (intrepid because many of the shots were taken when her knee was officially out of commission), but its first-line editor, clerk of the works, and tireless cheerleader. David is co-owner of the legendary Winooski Bike Shop in Winooski, Vermont. So great is its name that it operates without advertising, without display cases, without a bike in the window, without even a modest sign. David was the book's technical consultant, repair model (those are his grease-stained hands you see in the chapter on bike care), and front-line fact-checker.

A NOTE FROM THE AUTHOR

To the Person Reading This Standing Up in the Bookstore

I've got nothing against vertical perusal in a public publication empo-
rium. It's a long and honorable tradition, and it lets you know if this book
is one you want to add to your shopping basket or quietly slip back on the
shelf. So here's the lowdown on this book.

This is a book for real people. It is not for driven, shaved-legged racers, totally absorbed gearheads, or obsessive gram chasers (except to help
cure their obsession). If you're thinking of spending $9,000 on a fourth
bicycle, this book isn't for you.

Just who *is* this book for?

It's for people of all ages who share one or more of the following
views:

- It's wonderful to be outside.
- It's great to work your muscles without injuring yourself.
- It's good for you *and* planet Earth to get from point A to point B
  without engaging an internal combustion engine.
- It's a minor miracle to ride a bike that can eat up miles on the highway, snake through a pasture luminescent with golden dandelions,
  ford a rock-strewn stream, climb hills without causing a stroke, and
  handle dirt roads without knocking out all your fillings.

Backroad and offroad biking meets all those needs. It takes you where
you want to go. And I've tried to make this book the best place to start
the journey.

If you happen to be considering buying a bike in the near future, this
book can save you hundreds of dollars. More important, it can put you
on a bike you'll love for years instead of one that sits in the garage gathering dust.

CHAPTER 1

The Joys of Backroad and Offroad Biking

Backroad and offroad biking is, in my opinion, the greatest activity for the greatest number of people yet devised on our planet. But it is also the most misunderstood. Like cross-country skiing and snowboarding, it has been sold under the misleading term "mountain biking" as a sport for the superyoung, the superfit, and the hyperathletic. Bike magazines make this broad-ranging pastime look like it's composed almost entirely of jumping off high places or racing down the sides of cliffs. And it's true, you can do both those things on a mountain bike.

But in reality, the mountain bike's greatest contribution has been to make cycling fun for all. No more do you have to absorb every bump with your joints; the bike does it for you. No longer are you confined to paved roads; the knobby tires eat up dirt. Never again do you have to scrunch your internal organs between a horizontal chest and pumping knees; the relatively upright stance lets you breathe free. And with a mountain bike, you no longer have to face hills with dread; multiple gears handle the ups, and powerful brakes take care of the downs.

The mountain bike and its derivatives, known as hybrid bikes, are great vehicles for people of all ages, of nearly all levels of fitness. The combination of multiple gears, the rider's relatively upright position, and the big, shock-absorbing frame and tires make the mountain bike and its derivatives the vehicles of choice in nearly every geographic region. But both mountain bikes and hybrid bikes have been misunderstood, underappreciated, and underutilized by the general public, by real people.

•FAQ• On the side of my tires, it says "Inflate to 45 pounds." Should I always keep them at that pressure?

No. Many tires give you an inflation range, like 40–60 pounds. The 60 is for paved roads, 40 is for offroad, and you can adjust between them to get the right balance of comfort, glide, and grip for the day's cycling conditions. If you underinflate, you risk a flat and possible damage to the rim when the tire bottoms out against it. If you overinflate, you risk blowing the tire off the rim. Most manufacturers include a margin of safety in setting maximum pressure recommendations, but you don't want to be the one who finds out what it is. One more thing: Heavyweight riders need more air pressure than flyweights. So don't feel constrained to keep your tire right on the mark, especially if they give you only one mark to go on. ■

Prince Edward Island

If you're a backroad or offroad cyclist, it's hard to imagine a better two-wheeled vacation than Prince Edward Island. Most of the province is level or gently rolling, the weather tends to be maritime mild, and the roads (with a couple of serious exceptions near the Anne of Green Gables homestead) are both uncrowded and well maintained, making it ideal cycling country.

Early September is the ideal time to cycle Prince Edward Island. The bulk of the summer tourists have left. Days run from shirtsleeve warm to cardigan cool; nights are comforter cozy. The island's many live theaters are still open (they shut down one by one as the autumn calendar advances) and have plenty of seats. There are still music festivals, oyster festivals, cultural festivals, and children's festivals to enjoy. And though a fair number of museums and tearooms are closed for the season, prices on everything from inns to airfares to souvenirs tend to be lower than in high summer.

One of the best places to cycle is along the Confederation Trail. The Confederation is part of one of North America's best adaptations to change, the Rails to Trails movement, in which, throughout the continent, local groups have succeeded in turning unused railroad beds to recreation paths, primarily for the pleasure of bicyclers.

Nowhere has Rails to Trails been more successful than on Prince Edward Island. Even though the trail is still under construction, you can bike from one end of this 140-mile, smile-shaped island to the other. A good place to start is at the trail's eastern end, in tiny Mount Stewart.

There, at Trailside Cafe, you can rent a bike, taste fresh oyster stew, and take in live evening entertainment.

The entire trail can be comfortably handled on any kind of bike, though a mountain bike or hybrid is better than a racing or touring bike. It's the kind of terrain that families can enjoy together. Most of the trail is nearly flat and surfaced with compressed gravel. Its many gates and bridges are painted bright fuchsia. If you ride it on the right day, you may not encounter anyone the entire day.

The Morell–to–St. Peters section is a good example of the Confederation Trail's appeal. The track is easily wide enough for side-by-side cycling, very nearly flat, and paved with finely crushed stone. On the right of the trail are hayfields, copses of young poplars and old firs, and wildflowers. On the left is the water world.

The trail runs beside and over saltwater bogs, estuaries, and small bays. Markers for Prince Edward Island's famous mussel lines form white patterns on a blue bay. Great blue herons stand motionless by the shore, flying off as you approach. Gulls, terns, and crows wheel and dive. A lone Canada goose guards his portion of fishing ground. The only sounds, aside from the whir of rubber on gravel, are the cries of the gulls and the honk of the goose.

For cyclists who want to get from one section of the Confederation Trail to another, even in high season, most highways are free from the traffic of summer tourism. The King's Byway, Route 16, from the fishing town of St. Peters and the fishing village of Naufrage is typical. Between the white church spires of St. Peters to Naufrage's octagonal wooden lighthouse, the road runs through gently rolling farmland dotted with tidy white houses. Like much on this island province, it's a reminder of the way life can be lived in a rural, maritime, underpopulated place.

You also see signs of the island's peacefulness. Page four of the provincial paper, *The Guardian,* opened with a bold-faced headline, "Worker pricked by needle." The second story dealt with a Kmart employee who "used some security tape to mark an item and arranged to have it delivered to his home without paying for it."

Life is good. ■

CHAPTER 2

Buying and Fitting the Right Bike

Oh, how bikes have changed. Forget those old Schwinns and Columbias that weighed in at 75 pounds. Today's bikes are lighter, stronger, and better designed than any that went before. New ones are made of chromoly and aluminum alloy, carbon fiber and titanium. They are designed by computers, tested in wind tunnels, and built (depending on price and country of origin) by hi-tech welding specialists or robots.

All these improvements do come at a price, however. If you're not too heavy or hard-driving, you can get a serviceable ten-speed from your local discount store for under $90. That's an incredible bargain. But for anything fancier, expect to pay more. Top-of-the-line bikes can sell for as much as $15,000, but unless you're a racer, you don't need that much in a bike. As a rule, you're paying the big bucks for what's missing: weight. And while a light bike will give you more distance for the effort than a heavy one, unless you're a serious racer, shaving ounces doesn't make all that much difference. One could even argue that if you use a bike largely for exercise, you're doing yourself a favor by buying a relatively heavy one. You'll achieve more weight loss or muscle gain for the time and distance expended, and your dollar will go much farther.

Don't buy any bike without trying it first, even if all you can manage is a few turns around the shop parking lot. The first question to ask yourself is whether you feel comfortable on the bike. If not, keep looking.

The second question is whether a bike matches your cycling style. Be honest with yourself. Even if you picture yourself leaping over crags, if you live in Nebraska or Florida, you aren't going to encounter much of anything except level ground. So don't buy a climbing machine, buy a bike built for distance. Likewise, if you stay pretty much on pavement, don't buy a bike with huge, knobby tires. Look for a bike that matches most of the uses you'll put it to.

According to Greg Padley, a bike-industry expert, the best way to select a mountain bike is by taking one for a long test ride on the terrain where you'll be riding. Most bicycle companies offer dealers special pricing on demo and rental bikes, so your local bicycle dealer should have several options to choose from. It's in your best interests to test-ride them.

Bikes that have no suspension, known as *rigids,* and bikes without rear suspension, called *hardtails,* are fine for rails to trails, city streets, and bike paths. But for offroad riding, suspension allows you to ride farther faster and more comfortably. Properly designed suspension offers better traction and better braking. Full-suspension bicycles come in three varieties: cross-country, free ride, and downhill. Deciding which type of full-suspension bike is best depends on your intended style of riding.

- *Cross-country bikes* generally have a maximum of four inches of suspension travel. These bikes are fairly lightweight (24 to 30 pounds) and include enough gears to climb and descend mountainous terrain. Because cross-country bikes are designed to ascend as well as descend, they are the most efficient of the three suspension bike categories. For all but the most aggressive offroad rider, a cross-country bike is the best choice in full suspension.
- *Downhill bikes* are built with a single purpose in mind: to descend as quickly as possible. To this end, they have a limited gear range, up to 12 inches of suspension travel, and are overbuilt to survive torturous riding. Downhill design criteria make these expensive bikes heavy, inefficient climbers. If the only trail is down, this is the right bike for you.
- *Free-ride bikes* are a combination of cross-country and downhill models. The long-travel suspension and beefy frame of a gravity machine is combined with gears low enough to climb a mountain. These bikes are the summer choice of many ski-area rental shops because of the tough frame, long-travel suspension, and consumer-friendly gears. Free-ride bikes are usually those used by the high-flying, daredevil riders seen on TV commercials.

There is one other option: the single-speed mountain bike. One-speed riders claim to be more in touch with the terrain, their machines, and their bodies, and they don't have the worries and maintenance of multigear drivetrains. If you are strong or don't mind a little walking, a single speed's pure simplicity can't be beat. If you're not a purist, though, I'd go with gears.

OPPOSITE: **Racing: Anorexic tires.**

The bottom line is this: Mountain biking is fun. A bike from any of these categories will provide a good time. Choose the right bike for the right application, and you'll have a blast.

Those are the mountain bike choices—now comes the hard part. If you're like most—not all, but most—North Americans, the bike you want may not be a mountain bike, after all. Before we take this unusual line in a book that's essentially about mountain bikes, let us consider the beauty, the function, the wonder of the bicycle.

There is nothing like a bike. For getting from here to there under your own power, for really seeing a new town, for experiencing the countryside, for self-regulating, low-impact, multimuscle exercise, for spending time with the one you love, there is nothing like a bike.

Consider, if you will, seeing sights. Sightseeing from a bus is a poor way to see things; it's too hurried. Walking is too time-consuming. The bicycle, on the other hand, lets you see, exercise, see some more, stop and smell the honeysuckle, wander, see some more, stop for hardshell crabs and a pitcher of beer. Biking lets you absorb a place in a way no other means of transportation can.

What are the characteristics of the ideal bike for seeing what's around you? A fairly upright stance is number one. If you're hunched over your handlebars, you could miss the hummingbirds darting in and out of a leafy maple tree.

Second is a comfortable seat. Even the most beautiful sunset loses its glow if your butt hurts.

Third is a wide range of gears. You'll never see the three-state view from the top of the hill if you can't make it up the hill.

What kind of bikes combine upright posture, broad saddle, and full gearing? Mountain bikes. But a fair number—maybe even the majority— of mountain bikes don't. Because they're designed for racers and promoted as wheeled racehorses, they have low, flat handlebars and high seatposts, forcing you into a more aerodynamic but less comfortable and less viewable riding position.

If you're a mountain bike racer, that position is just what you need. If not, it's the last thing you need. Rather, you want a bike built for comfort, not for speed. You want high handlebars instead of flat ones, a broad and padded saddle, and tires that can handle the highway as well as the streambed. As the market now stands, you want a bike despised by purists, grudgingly shown by young male salesmen, and produced only reluctantly by manufacturers. You want a hybrid.

Mountain bike

Hybrid bike

The hybrid bike, also called a city bike or lifestyle bike, doesn't handle paved roads as well as a racing bike. It doesn't handle rocky streambeds as well as a mountain bike. But it handles both adequately, and it handles the broad in-between better than either. You can take it with aplomb through fields, over dirt roads, along an old logging track, up steep switchbacks, down a defile. You can ride it long distances with comfort. You can see the hummingbirds, smell the coffee, enjoy the ride.

What are the differences between a mountain bike and a hybrid? The mountain bike has fatter tires, a heavier frame, and, usually, 26-inch wheels. The hybrid has 27-inchers or Euro 700 Cs, which are a little smaller than the 27s but bigger than the 26s. The smaller ones are better for climbing steep hills and for handling deep mud. They're also stronger, which is important when plowing through rocky ravines, less so when cruising backroads. The larger hybrid tires are faster on roads and take less pedal energy to make them turn.

If you spend a significant amount of time on steep and muddy paths, a mountain bike is for you. If you're spending most of your time on paved or dirt roads, give serious consideration to the hybrid. If you live in a city other than, say, San Francisco or New York, you want a hybrid. (San Francisco because of the hills; New York because of the streets. As the *New York Times* put it, "Many city cyclists choose a mountain bike for ordinary street riding since the pot-holed pavement and kamikaze traffic present a fair approximation of wilderness obstacles.")

Because my hybrid hypothesis—that most mountain bike buyers would be better off with a hybrid—is so different from the position taken by most writers, I thought I'd better put it to the test. Our annual North Hatley, Quebec, ride gave me the perfect opportunity.

North Hatley is one of those perfect towns for a summer cycling vacation. It's on a gorgeous lake, is filled with antique and craft shops, and comes with a French ambience just a few miles north of the U.S. border. What's more, it's the start of an extraordinary bike loop. Over the course of about 30 miles, the loop follows an old railroad track, passes an abandoned copper mine, runs along a scenic river, winds through woods, meanders through the streets (with clearly marked bike lanes) of a small city, and occasionally hugs the edge of a country highway. It has long stretches of level ground, some serious uphills, fast-paced downhills, and a fair number of tight S-curves. Surfaces vary from asphalt road and cement sidewalk to gravel, rutted dirt, and occasional rough riding, especially if there's construction. It includes almost every condition most mountain bikers are likely to encounter.

Most years I do it on my mountain bike, either the old $225 model or the new $800 one. This year I did it on a $250, five-year-old hybrid. For one 5-mile section I switched bikes and rode a high-level mountain bike. Here's what I found.

On the long uphills, the really rough surfaces, and the occasional loose gravel, I preferred the mountain bike; on the hybrid, I missed those extralow gears and extrafat tires. But for much of the trip, I preferred the hybrid. The upright position was much easier on my arms than the flat handlebars of the high-end mountain bike, and the relatively skinny tires rolled with less resistance. All in all, the two bikes came out roughly even.

The next week, I went to the New England Mountain Bike Festival in Randolph, Vermont. An entire forest was converted into mountain bike trails, which were designed for maximum contact with slurping mud, impossible inclines, root-and-rock-strewn paths through tree and pucker-brush. It was great fun on a mountain bike, a disaster on a hybrid.

Sometimes a mountain bike is the vehicle of choice.

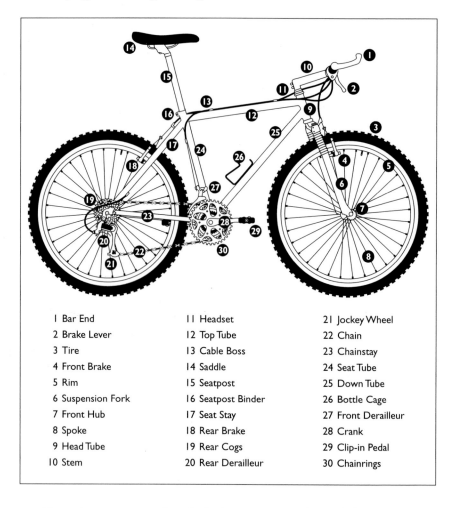

1 Bar End	11 Headset	21 Jockey Wheel
2 Brake Lever	12 Top Tube	22 Chain
3 Tire	13 Cable Boss	23 Chainstay
4 Front Brake	14 Saddle	24 Seat Tube
5 Rim	15 Seatpost	25 Down Tube
6 Suspension Fork	16 Seatpost Binder	26 Bottle Cage
7 Front Hub	17 Seat Stay	27 Front Derailleur
8 Spoke	18 Rear Brake	28 Crank
9 Head Tube	19 Rear Cogs	29 Clip-in Pedal
10 Stem	20 Rear Derailleur	30 Chainrings

Keep these two tests in mind when you go to buy a bike. Try to honestly gauge how much time you're likely to spend on major steeps, rocky single track, or deep mud. Then decide whether to spend your money on a mountain bike or a hybrid.

FEATURES
You'll face several decisions as you peruse the bikes in the shop.

Materials
Bike frames can be made of steel, aluminum, titanium, or composite. Unless you have cash to burn, you can eliminate titanium and composite. Steel is a bit heavier, more flexible, and cheaper than aluminum. The aluminum

Grip Shift

used in most bike frames is stiffer, which often translates to more efficient but less shock-absorbing. Highly successful frames have been made of each, and both have loyal adherents. Try before you buy.

Shifters

The bicycle is constantly evolving. Today's mountain bikes are better than those of a decade ago, and all bikes are superior to the one you had growing up. Nowhere has the evolution been more pronounced than in the gears and shifters, and the most significant change has been the development of index shifting. Instead of having to find the right gear by feathering the shift lever back and forth until the grinding stops, index shifting means that each time you click the shifter, the chain moves one gear.

The best-known names in index shifting are Grip Shift and Rapid-Fire. Grip Shift lets you shift simply by twisting the handlebar grip; Rapid-Fire requires thumb work. Grip Shift is lighter and maybe not quite as robust.

Rapid-Fire shifter

By and large, beginners prefer Grip Shift and experienced cyclists like Rapid-Fire. If you have signs of carpal tunnel syndrome or Repetitive Strain Injury (RSI), I'd avoid the twisting motion that Grip Shift requires. Again, try before you buy.

Suspension

Over the past decade, another major change in mountain bike design is the availability of suspension systems. Their purpose, like the shocks on your car, is to provide a more comfortable ride. So the advantage of suspension is that it reduces the shocks that

Front shocks

come from riding rough trails. With fewer jolts, you can stay in the seat rather than stand on the pedals when riding over bone-jarring ruts and rocks. That saves energy. But suspension systems add weight to a bike. Weight costs energy. If you're a lightweight, carrying the extra pounds around is going to tire you out. And a suspension system adds more than weight; it adds to the price and adds more cost in the form of maintenance.

So should you buy a softtail bike or an unsuspended hardtail? I say, shell out the extra bucks, live with the extra pounds, and get the bounce. Why? Aside from my own experience, which strongly favors suspension, a recent study by Ezekial Tan concluded that the offroad jarring transmitted through the handlebars to the wrists can lead to nonfracture injuries. The study also concluded that having front suspension is the most important safety measure mountain bikers can take to prevent wrist injuries. Some bike riders, who dismissed their wrist injuries as simple strains, are developing degenerative arthritis of the wrist after a few years. Mountain bikers also reported that wearing padded gloves helped prevent wrist pain.

If you're committed to a bike without rear suspension, you can still get some of the benefits at a lower price and with less weight with a suspension seatpost. They range from $25 to about $150, and they're a lot better than nothing.

If you're going to get shocks (and unless you're a flyweight or a purist, I recommend you do), get both front and rear suspension. Have more fun. Save your fillings. But if you're counting pennies, front shocks are better than no shocks; they'll save your arms, if not your back.

Brakes

Mountain bike brakes have always been much more efficient stopping tools than road bike brakes. In

A suspension seatpost is a reasonable alternative to a full-suspension bike.

recent years, they've gotten even better, especially on moderate and high-end models. One of the things you get when you pay more for a cycle is more powerful, responsive brakes. Direct-pull brakes, also called V-brakes, stop you in a shorter time with less effort than the cantilever brakes that they have largely replaced. And now some bike companies are putting disk brakes, like the ones on sports cars, on mountain bikes. These brakes will stop on a dime, but for most riders, they are overkill, both in price and power. Direct-pull brakes are effective enough for almost anything, and even most cantilever brakes are solid stopping machines. The one great advantage to disk brakes is that they save the wheel rim. For hard riders who put on a lot of miles, the regular pressure of brake pad against rim wears them both down. Brake pads are cheap; rim replacement isn't. Since disk brakes make no contact with the rim, they will save you that expense and chore.

Kickstand

Kickstands are really convenient, and you won't waste time at every stop trying to figure out where to lay your expensive bike down in the dirt, but they weigh a couple pounds. Some riders leave off the kickstand, not wanting to lug an extra 2 pounds up hills and down. Kickstands are for kids they say, not for serious riders.

I say get the stand. When you go on a long, hilly trip, unscrew it, which takes about a minute and a half. It takes only another two minutes to screw it back on.

Handlebars

Most mountain bikes have flat or raised handlebars. Hybrids sometimes come with curved-down bars, the kind you find on racing and touring bikes. If most of your travel is going to be long-distance road work—say, more than 10 or 15 miles at a stretch—the curved-down handlebars can be a good choice. They give you more ways to shift position: down on the grips, up on the bars, farther up on the brake levers. Changing positions eases shoulder and neck strain and, for some, outweighs the added strain of horizontal riding. All that position changing has another positive effect: After a long trip, your rear end isn't nearly as sore. Another advantage of touring bars is that they cut your wind resistance. The downside is that they put you in a more extreme position, stretched out over the bars. If you know from experience that your shoulders ache when you ride, you may want to consider another style of handlebars.

According to David Nesbitt, trailmaster at the Balsams Grand Resort Hotel in Dixville Notch, New Hampshire, "Flat handlebars stretch you out a bit more and are very good for technical woods riding. The flat bars allow considerable leverage to lift the front wheel over rocks and roots on the trail. Riser, or raised, handlebars are for either recreational or downhill applications. The recreational cyclist can sit more upright in style and comfort. The downhill racer likes these bars for the shorter reach, allowing more shock absorption and better viewing of steep decent at high speeds. The downside is that leverage is lost, so it's harder to loft over obstacles."

Nesbitt's favorite handlebars are "the Mustache bars, which look like drop bars flared out to the sides. Mustache bars are multipositional and allow numerous places to rest the hands. They are comfortable for long rides and really help on hill climbs, as their width opens the rider's chest to facilitate breathing. I find the Mustache handlebars the most versatile I have ever used, and they grace three of my bikes. They're made by Nitto of Japan and distributed through your local bike shop or via the Rivendale catalog."

There are two other alternatives. For not much money—starting at around $20—you can buy a set of bar ends that attach to the handlebars. These give you not only a second hold-on position, but also extra power climbing hills. Almost everyone who tries them likes them. The downside of bar ends is that they may cause back stress. Another option is to buy an add-on, a set of drop bars that attach to mountain bike handlebars. This gives you the best of both worlds; the only downsides are added weight and expense.

Touring bars make long rides more comfortable.

Bar ends give extra power on hill climbs.

Saddles

The bike part that's potentially hardest on your body is the saddle. Not only can it be uncomfortable, it can do you real damage. Even seats that claim to be designed to reduce damage may cause problems.

I recommend padding, but not too much padding. On long hauls, the purist's hard and narrow saddle gets old fast. The trouble with too much padding is that, like a too-soft mattress, it can lead to body problems later.

The saddle should be wide, but not too wide. Though a rail isn't a comfortable perch, the saddle shouldn't be so wide that it chafes your thighs every time you pedal. Find a happy medium that works for you.

Consider trying a saddle with a hole in it. Theoretically, it should relieve pressure on some sensitive points, but having tried one and talked to women who also have, I'm not entirely convinced. You could wait for conclusive studies, or you could try before you buy by trading saddles with

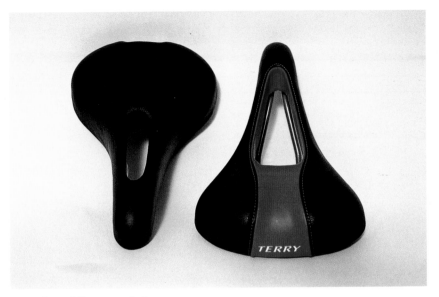

Protective saddles are made for women
(left) and men (right).

friends. Borrow a seat for a morning's ride and see how you like it. If you do, expect to pay from $20 to well over $100 for such a saddle.

One task of a bike shop is to get customers comfortable on the bike they just bought. The most frequent point of discomfort is the saddle. According to David Porter of Vermont's Winooski Bike Shop, "Most of the people that we see here with 'saddle' problems actually have a positioning problem. Usually it's that the saddle is too high. That's why I don't think very highly of the Band-Aid solution that gel pads, sheepskin covers, holes in the saddle, and spring-loaded seatposts represent. Resolving the fundamental position problem usually solves the saddle problem."

This saddle is too low. There's too much bend in the rider's knee.

Now it's too high. See how her feet are stretched.

Here the saddle's about right. Ride and adjust until it's to your liking.

How high should your seat be? Most riders believe that your legs should have a slight bend in them when the pedal is in the down position, but Effin and I prefer a straight leg. Here's how to determine the best height for you: If your hips start hurting when you ride, shorten the seatpost by half an inch. If your knees start hurting, lengthen it by half an inch.

To prevent chafing from the saddle, wash both your shorts and the body parts they cover often and thoroughly. To prevent worsening of chafing, apply a lotion containing lanolin to those same parts.

Tires

The odds are very high that you'll buy the tires that come with the bike. But as with so many other components, you can negotiate, and you may be able to get the salesman to switch those tires for a pair more suited to your needs. You want the width and tread that best match your style of cycling. If you plan to spend most of your time on pavement, go narrower and smoother. This will give you the best roll, letting you go farther faster and with less effort. If you'll be climbing rocky trails in the woods, go wider and knobbier. You'll do less slipping and sliding, and you'll probably be fixing fewer flats.

Speaking of flats, you may find yourself tempted to buy tubeless, flatproof tires. They're cheap, they're solid, and they'll never blow. Sounds too good to be true? It's all true, but while they're better made than they used to be, they still don't roll like a pneumatic tire. And since rolling is what you do on a bike, I'd avoid them until they run as sweetly as their air-filled cousins. For now, better stick with the pneumatic models.

Another choice you'll face is that of tire valves. In North America, there are two kinds: Presta and Schraeder. Schraeder is the kind used on car tires. Presta valves are made for bikes. It's easier to fill a Presta because there's no resistance when you pump it up. It also has fewer parts and is preferred by gearheads. Which valve do I prefer? I prefer taking the one that comes with the bike. Having used both with no trouble, I see no reason to waste brain cells over the matter. Whichever valve you choose, it's best to inflate it with a hand pump, not the one at the gas station, which is faster but considerably more likely to blow up your tube.

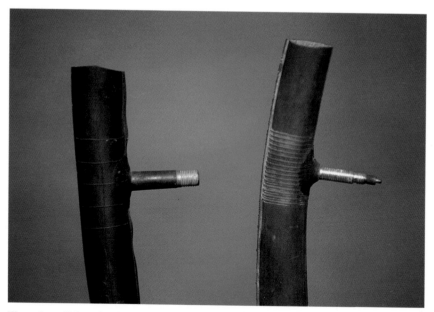

Tire valves: Schraeder (left) and Presta. For most cyclists, either will do just fine.

Pedals

Some bikes come with pedals; some don't. Either way, through checkbook or negotiation, you can choose pedals on your own. You have three choices: plain platform, toeclip, or clipless. Here's how they stack up:

Platform, or Plain Pedal. Made of steel, plastic, or old-fashioned rubber, this is the kind of pedal that came on your Schwinn when you were ten. Mountain bike models have a grippier, more rugged surface, but they're all just a place to put your foot.

Upside: It's cheap and takes no getting used to.

Downside: It's much less efficient than the other choices, and it encourages pedaling from the relatively weak arch rather than the more robust ball of the foot.

Toeclip, or Rat-trap. The toeclip consists of a plastic or metal cage and strap for the front of your foot attached to a platform pedal.

Upside: It's cheap, starting at under $5, and when pedaling, you can lift against the clip to get power on the upstroke as well as the down.

Downside: For some, the confinement is frightening at first. If cinched too tight, toeclips can cut off circulation. They're awkward to get into. Getting out in a hurry takes practice. And if you find yourself accidentally pedaling on the bottom side of the pedal as you weave through

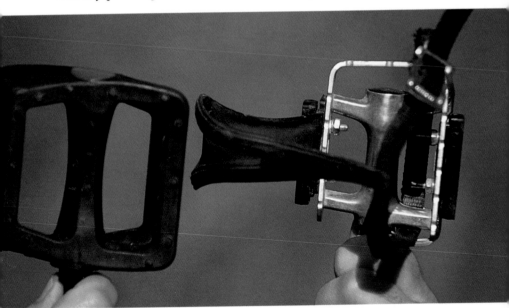

Two kinds of platform pedals; the one on the right has a toeclip.

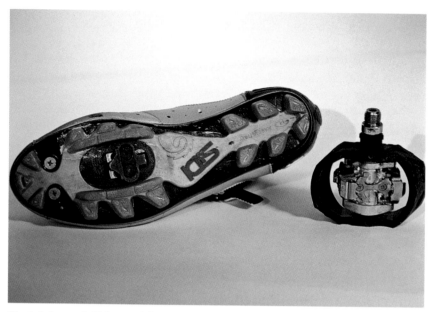

Cleated shoe and clipless pedal.

SIDI and Shimano bike shoes.

the woods, that hanging cage and strap can snag a rock and bring you to earth.

Clipless, or Clip-in. With clipless pedals, a cleat in the sole of your special-made shoe locks into what looks like a pedal stripped of its platform. Those special-made shoes come with either recessed or exposed cleats. Recessed cleats are for offroad biking, exposed, for road biking. Since you can barely walk in exposed cleats, and since offroad biking (as well as the rest of life) often requires walking, always buy recessed.

Upside: This is the most efficient connection yet devised between foot and bike. Once you've practiced, they're easy to get in and out of, even in a hurry.

Downside: You have to buy shoes you can't use for anything but biking. The pedals go for $40 to $250 and the shoes for $60 to $220. Getting out in a hurry takes practice and, at least at first, nerve.

I've tried all three options, and my strong advice is to get either toeclips or clipless pedals; plain old platform pedals rob you of too much power, stability, and pleasure. It's hard to try clipless before you buy, but at most bike stores you can try toeclips. If they're adjustable, don't cinch them tight; that way you can relax as you're getting used to them. Better still, on those first toeclip rides, don't even use the straps. The clips themselves will keep your feet on the pedals, and without the straps, there's no impediment to fast exits.

To save money on shoes, and if you don't bike too long or too hard, clips are fine. For the best ride, I recommend clipless, but only with shoes you can walk in.

This is not a universal view, even in my own home. Effin finds clipless pedals way too confining. She went down once—a slow, almost balletic fall that left bruises on her hand, arm, calf, and thigh—and she had those new pedals off the bike ten minutes later. I went down twice, but I love the efficiency so much, I figure it's worth the learning curve—and the occasional pain. Whether using toeclips or clipless pedals, I slip or click out of them whenever I'm barreling down an unpaved road or weaving through too-close trees. As I'm getting more comfortable with the clipless pedals, however, I'm gradually staying in them longer on dicey ground. David Porter, bike guru and co-owner of Winooski Bicycle Shop, goes further: "Above all else, I want to keep that top tube from coming into contact with my sensitive parts. The last thing I want is to come bouncing off the bike and end up straddling the tube. So I make sure I'm solidly clipped in when the going gets rough."

Some cyclists will do anything to shave an extra gram.

FRAME SIZE AND BIKE WEIGHT

More pages of bike books, magazines, and catalogs have been devoted to frame size than just about any other subject. There are formulas, measurement systems, and equations for getting exactly the right frame for you. Many even argue that the problem is so great, you should have the frame custom built to fit your body.

If you're in any way different from the average shape, a custom frame will fit you better than an off-the-rack model. It will take into account your long arms and short torso, for example, as well as your height and weight. If you're a 100-pounder, you won't have to tote around as much frame weight as one built for your 220-pound cousin. The frame will be made to your specs, designed to meet your needs, and probably outfitted with the components—type of brakes, number and range of gears, width of saddle—you choose. But such a bike will probably cost you about $4,000.

Bike weight is what separates driven cyclists from the rest of the world. The driven cyclist is, first and foremost, a gram chaser. If he can shave a gram by drilling little holes in the seatpost, you can guarantee that's how he'll be spending the next few nights. If she can cut 2 grams by buying a set of $500 pedals, that's what she's saving her pennies for.

Unless you are an aspiring racer or an ultra-long-distance rider, you don't need to be overly concerned about bike weight. For most of us, biking is simply a way to get around, to chalk up exercise time, to enjoy the

outdoors, and to have fun. You can accomplish all this on a one-speed land cruiser, a second-hand clunker, or that old Columbia in your mother's garage. You'll likely have even more fun on a hybrid or mountain bike, but you don't have to turn into a fanatic to do so. As for weight, buy the lightest model that suits your needs (a hybrid will weigh less than an ultra-rugged mountain bike) and that falls within your price range.

•FAQ• **Where should I buy my bike?**

Here's some advice from Kate Carter, the founding editor of *Vermont Sports Today* and author of *Mountain Bike Vermont:*

First-time bicycle shoppers might be tempted by four-color newspaper inserts advertising department store bicycles for $199. The price seems reasonable, and bicycles are all pretty much the same, aren't they? They all have two wheels, a saddle, brakes, handlebars, and maybe some gears for the hills. So why pay more?

Because there is a lot more to buying a bicycle than price. If you want a bike you can happily ride for years, consider these three things: fit, reparability, and service.

Only a bike shop, where they sell and service bicycles every day, can give you all three. But not for $199. Most likely you will spend twice that. Although $400 might sound excessive for your first bicycle, it's worth every cent when you consider what you get—a bicycle that fits you, that can be easily repaired, and that can be serviced by the mechanic at the shop where you bought it or at any other bike shop.

Proper fit is essential so that your bike will remain comfortable on long rides and your cycling will not be hampered by strained and stressed body parts. Most bike shops have bike-fitting kits or measurement formulas that calculate the size you need. The bike's toptube and seattube should be proportioned to fit your torso and leg measurements.

Bikes need both parts and service now and then. The shop where you buy your bike has replacement parts in stock. It also has the personnel and tools to do the job.

So the next time you are tempted by colorful ads showing bikes for under $199, remember that what you see is what you get. Nothing more, and maybe a lot less. Definitely not enough. Throw out the flyer and pay a

OPPOSITE: Kate Carter, author of *Mountain Bike Vermont,*
on her top-of-the-line titanium mountain bike.

visit to your local bike shop. While you're there, be sure to check out the $2,000 bikes—just to put things in perspective. ▨

GETTING THE RIGHT SIZE BIKE

Fitting, or sizing, is a dark and arcane art. As I peruse fitting techniques, sizing kits, and the theories of the gurus of the art, I think the process owes more to Merlin than to Einstein. Here's the technique employed by one shop:

> For bike sizing and preliminary saddle height determination, the shop uses an inseam measurement obtained thusly: Stand in stocking feet, thighs 1 1/2 inches apart. A broomstick is placed between the legs (feet 6 inches apart) and held in a position of direct solid contact with the crotch. While the contact should be solid, it should not be so extreme as to produce a wedgie. (A wedgie is what you have when someone yanks the back of the waistband of your undershorts.) Measure from the crotch to the floor. Multiply that times .883. Set the distance from the top of the saddle to the center of the bottom bracket to the resulting dimension.

Call me old-fashioned, but that seems a little complex for most folks I know. While most experts agree that a mountain bike should allow 2 to 3 inches of clearance between your crotch and the top tube, to ensure that they never meet during a quick dismount, from there on, they all seem to have their own way of determining the best fit. To make matters worse, there is no industry-wide standard for stating bike sizes. Amazing though it sounds, one brand's 20-inch bike may be significantly different from another's.

My own technique for bike fitting is a lot less complex: Get on the bike. If it feels weird, get off. If it feels good, ride it around the parking lot. If it still feels good, ride it up and down a couple of hills. If it still feels good, buy it before somebody else does.

Fitting women riders is often a little more involved. As trailmaster David Nesbitt explains:

> Every bike should properly fit the rider for comfort and safety; this sometimes takes a little more effort for the female rider, but the results are very much worth it. To begin with, female cyclists should have a proper woman's saddle. Since a woman's pelvis is wider than a man's, the

For a comfortable fit, this cyclist is too extended over the handlebars.

Now she's in a better-balanced position.

standard-issue saddle is usually a poor fit. A woman's saddle is shorter and wider so that bones and not soft tissue support the rider's weight. Another important feature is a cut-out under the nose of the saddle. When the rider leans forward, it eliminates pressure on sensitive areas.

The other important issue is reach. The average woman has longer legs and a shorter torso than a man. This results in her being able to ride a taller frame, but being unable to comfortably reach the handlebars. This causes sore hands, neck, and shoulders.

There are two ways to fix this problem: a shorter stem or a shorter top tube. A stem change takes just a few minutes and reels the handlebars in to a closer, more comfortable reach.

Terry Precision Bicycles for Women builds the best women's bikes, with a lot of attention to detail for the female cyclist. Terry also produces the best women's saddles on the market.

Physical therapist Phil Sweet emphasizes the importance of a proper fit to avoid injuries.

By its construction and design, the bicycle forces the rider into a pattern of movement that his body may not tolerate. After long hours in the saddle, the rider may end up with an overuse injury like a muscle strain or tendinitis. Instead of forcing your body to fit the bike, the bicycle should be changed to accommodate your body. If necessary, change the handlebar width, stem height, or saddle position, or buy a new saddle or a different kind of handlebars. You can also buy special pedals. Speedplay makes the most free-floating pedal available, but many companies make similar pedals. Let the bike shop salesman know you are looking for a pedal with maximum float.

In extreme circumstances, the bike frame may simply be wrong, but rarely is a new frame required. Frame size problems can easily be avoided if you have a formal fitting done at the bike shop before you buy a bike.

MAIL-ORDER BICYCLES

You may have disregarded my advice to try before you buy, or you may have found the right bike at your local bike store and then discovered you could save $14 tax if you ordered it from a catalog. Either way, your bike arrives disassembled in a box. Should you assemble it yourself, or take it to your local bike shop and pay to have it done?

Unless you love to tinker and have a lot of time and a well-equipped workroom, my strong advice is to let the bike shop mechanics do it. They have the specialized tools and a bike stand (the cycling equivalent of a vise); you probably don't. And the odds are your new bike got banged around in transit; they can both spot and repair misaligned brakes, wheels out of true, loose headsets, and other problems that you might miss.

And there's one more thing. According to bike shop owner David Porter.

> If you assemble the bike yourself and eventually realize there's something wrong with it and take it to a shop, they may not be delighted to see you, as they don't know what assembly procedures you followed. On the other hand, if you have your boxed bike assembled at a good shop, where they follow certain procedures in order to maximize function and long life of the bike's components, the shop is usually willing to take responsibility for it in the future.

BIKES FOR THE TRAVELING CYCLISTS

The ideal bike for the air traveler or the office commuter is small enough to fold into a suitcase and fit in a crowded elevator. Such bikes have existed for a long time, but most of them were mediocre to terrible to ride. But in 1992, Alan and Hans Scholz, owners of Green Gear Cycling, came up with Bike Friday, a performance cycle that collapses into a suitcase. They make mountain bike and hybrid models, each one fitted to the needs and size of individual purchasers. With their small wheels, they look toy-like, but I know cyclists who have taken them over the Alps and raced them through triathlons. There are other custom manufacturers who, through the use of a high-tech coupling from a company called S&S, also produce fine collapsible bikes.

BIKES OF THE FUTURE

While bikes have changed considerably in recent years—index shifting, suspension systems, better brakes—they don't change as fast as computers. Last year's model will serve you well this year. And next.

Still, it's nice to have an idea of where things are going, what the bike of the near future will look like. According to Greg Padley, who's a pro mountain bike racer, bike mechanic, and freelance writer, there are six areas of change.

More Gears

Component giant Shimano introduced Mega-9 and Mega-Range gearing systems in 1999. Mega-9 is a nine-speed cassette that, when combined with a triple crank, offers twenty-seven speeds. Currently, Mega-9 is top shelf stuff. However, Shimano's history of trickle-down technology foreshadows twenty-seven speeds throughout its line in the not-too-distant future. And that's not all. Later in the year, Italian component manufacturer Campagnolo upped the ante with a ten-speed road cassette and shifter.

Different Gears

In an effort to provide a more enjoyable ride for infrequent cyclists, Shimano's entry-level Mega-Range cassette employs a large, thirty-four-tooth cog. This offers one superlow, "bail-out" gear. In another new direction, French component manufacturer Mavic introduced an electronic rear shifter and derailleur that is truly push-button shifting. Check out www.mavic.com for updates.

Old-New Hubs

Shimano and its competitors, Sachs and Rohloff, are now making internally geared rear hubs like those on the three-speed English racers of yore. The new versions offer a wider gear selection and more reliable function. As the internally geared hub market continues to grow, expect further developments in this area.

More Brakes

Linear pull brakes, originally an expensive upgrade, are now offered on nearly every mountain bike. As offroad speeds have increased, even stronger brakes are being demanded. Hydraulic and cable-actuated disk brakes, like those from specialty manufacturers Hayes and Formula, are becoming more affordable as Asian companies enter the market. Just as suspension has taken nearly a decade to be accepted, these fancy brakes, once fully understood and accepted, will complement all offroadworthy bicycles.

More Suspension

As full-suspension bicycle designs become more refined and suspension components more affordable, expect to see more fully suspended bikes on the trail. Suspension seatposts have also made a big splash: The number of shock-absorbing seatpost manufacturers has tripled in three years.

As further proof of suspension's success, these posts are available as original equipment on many bikes.

More Comfort

As U.S. bike riders get older, bicycle and component manufacturers are working to capture returning and casual cyclists. To that end, lower gears, more comfortable seats, upright handlebars, and plusher suspensions are in vogue. So-called comfort bikes forgo the uncomfortable racing motif and feature many pampering upgrades as original equipment. At the extreme end, electric-assisted bikes are growing in popularity, especially in the Sunbelt, where retirees live in large numbers.

Mansion Peeping

Palm Beach, Florida, doesn't sound like it would have much in the way of biking *or* backroads. It is, after all, flatter than a bowling alley, richer than Donald Trump (actually, The Donald owns a sweet little palace there), older than Strom Thurmond, and more devoid of backroads than most places on earth.

But Palm Beach teaches a lesson. For if you can find backroad biking even in Palm Beach, you can find it just about anywhere. And you can, indeed, find it in Palm Beach.

Like many towns on the east coast of south Florida, Palm Beach is bounded on one side by the Atlantic Ocean and on the other by the Intracoastal Waterway, a broad canal that sometimes widens into lakes and bays and carries thousands of pleasure boats, tour boats, cargo boats, and work boats up and down its palm-lined banks. Although George Washington dreamed of an intracoastal waterway, a U.S. water passage safe from Atlantic storms, it was not completed until 1936. By then, the well-developed rail system had made it an anachronism for commerce. But as U.S. waterways switched from transportation to recreation, the safe inland passage came into its own.

Today you can pedal along this historic waterway, starting from downtown Palm Beach. No cars, no trucks, no diesel smell or honking horns—just a few cyclists, an in-line skater or two, a jogger, an old couple strolling. The smells are of salt water and mown grass. The sounds are the *whoosh* of tires, the *whirrr* of skate wheels, the panting of a tired jogger. Pelicans fly overhead and sit perched on wharf railings.

And there's entertainment as well. The yachts of the ultrarich ply these waters and tie up beside the path. The homes (in many cases, second, third, or fourth homes) of the yacht owners sit on the other side of the path. Both allow wonderful opportunities for snooping. The path serves as the border of the front yards of these Spanish-style mansions, offering an excellent view.

And you don't even have to take your own bike. Half a dozen area shops rent cycles at reasonable rates. What more could you ask? ■

CHAPTER 3

Accessories, Gear, and Clothing

What You Need and What You Don't

What accessories do you need on a backroad or offroad bike? Few, really. They fall into two categories: stuff for the body and stuff for the bike.

ACCESSORIES

You need a mirror, a pump, reflectors, and if you ever bike at dawn, dusk, or night, a light. A bell is good if you bike in the city. That's really about all. You can add lots more, including speedometer, odometer, heart-rate monitor, luggage rack, panniers, mudguards, and a dozen other objects that are useful and could be fun, but you can also live quite happily without them.

Mirror

You need a mirror to see what's coming up behind you. A logging truck, for instance. There are four kinds of mirrors from which to choose.

- A mirror that fits on your helmet or glasses is always there when you need it, but it may be too small and close for good vision, and you may not like having extra plastic or glass that near your eye.
- A big, long-stemmed mirror that screw-clamps over your handlebars is cheap and gives you a great view, but it looks geeky and is wind-resistant.
- A mirror that screws into the end of your handlebars has a bigger surface and is far from your eyes, but when the handlebars are turning, all you see is trees.
- A mirrow held with Velcro on the end of your handlebars costs less than the screw-on type and has the same advantages, but it slips down the bar at every bump and you can't see a thing.

Having tried them all, the worst I've found is the Velcro model. My choice is a screw-in with a wide-angle mirror. The long-stemmed kind probably works even better, but even I have limits to geekiness.

A word of caution about mirrors: Don't rely on them. Consider your mirror an early-warning system, but before you make that left turn on a busy highway, look over your shoulder as well. Assume your mirror has blind spots, and remember, a cyclist is a frail and vulnerable creature, especially in traffic.

Pump

I'll admit it from the start—I don't carry a pump. I have a floor pump at home, and it has an adapter to fit both types of valve stems, but I don't carry a pump when I ride.

You should. If you carry a pump and a small, lightweight tire repair kit, you'll never have to push a bike home because you couldn't fix a simple flat.

Most experienced tire repairers advise buying as big a pump as you can comfortably carry so you don't spend as much time inflating the tire as you would walking it home. And almost everyone buys a frame-fit pump that attaches to the bike so you don't have to wear a backpack to carry the pump. An alternative is a CO_2 pump, which is small enough to

The bottom mirror is held on by Velcro, the middle is screwed in, and the big one on top fits over the bars.

fit in your pocket and uses CO_2 cartridges to inflate the tire. Innovations in Cycling makes a couple of popular models that sell for about $20. Floor pumps start around $20, frame-fits around $15.

Here's a good pump tip: Instead of lubricating your pump with petroleum oil, which will rot the pump's rubber parts, use castor oil, available at your local drugstore.

Light and Reflectors

If you bike at night, in the city or country, you need a light and reflectors. Reflective clothing is also a good investment. I rarely bike at night, but whenever I go off alone, I take along a blinking light, as much to help the rescuers find me as to help drivers avoid me. No, I've never had to use it, but I feel better knowing it's there. And apply reflectors generously: to your wheels, mudguards, clothing, and pedals. On wheels and pedals, they're especially effective, since their constant motion quickly gets drivers' attention. While you can buy a light for under $20, you can also spend well over $200 for a big bright one.

Bell

Especially if you cycle in the city, a bike bell, just like the one you had as a kid, is a good way of letting folks know you are there. They worked then; they still do.

BIKE RACKS

If you travel with your bike, unless you own a minivan or pickup truck, you'll need a bike rack. Although there are many brands, when it comes down to it, there are only two kinds of bike racks: those that go on the back of the car and those that go on top. Each has its plusses and minuses.

Top-loading Racks

Top-loaders hold bikes very securely, preventing them from rubbing against each other or rubbing the paint off the car. They're a bit more secure against theft than rear racks. And most of them can handle up to four bikes at a time. The downside is that you've got to get those bikes on the roof. If you're weak or short or have a tall vehicle, this may be close to impossible without a loved one and/or a stepstool. Many owners of sport utility vehicles always carry a stool with them. Top-loaders aren't cheap; expect to pay $100 to $300. Another disadvantage of the top-loader is that one fine day you'll drive merrily into your garage, forgetting that the bikes are up there, and hear the most awful crunching sound you ever heard.

Rear-end Racks

Rear-enders come in two models: the kind you strap to your trunk and the kind you snap into your trailer hitch. These racks are a lot more convenient and easy to load than the top-loaders. You can hoist up to three bikes on them (four on the hitch models) without raising your hands above your head. The trunk loaders are also considerably simpler than the top-loaders, which translates to considerably cheaper, starting around $50. The downside is that it's not easy to get into your trunk when 90 pounds of steel and rubber are blocking the lid. On a long trip, the bikes can abrade each other. But worst of all is that one fine day, you'll be slipping through a narrow opening between two parked cars and hear the most awful crunching sound . . .

CLOTHING AND OTHER ACCESSORIES

You need padded bike shorts, padded gloves, sunglasses, water carrier, and most important, a helmet.

Watch your head.

Watch your back.

Padded Shorts

I don't care if they make your butt look fat, you need padded shorts. Cycling involves a lot of sitting on a small, hard seat. Get some padding between you and the seat. If you hate the way regular bike shorts look, you can buy models that look like ordinary shorts with padding installed. But don't skimp on that padding; it will mean the difference between a pleasant evening and a night of pain. Expect to spend $20 to $90 for bike shorts.

Wash your bike shorts with ordinary soap or Ivory Snow, not detergent. For sensitive skin, the detergent residue could cause sores, particularly on the inner thighs.

Another thing that helps is a padded seat cover. If that still isn't enough, many contemporary saddle makers are offering bike seats with built-in padding. Slipping a padded seat cover over a padded seat attached to a shock-absorbing seat stem on a fat-tired, full-suspension bike is as close to butt heaven as you'll ever find.

Cycling guides often recommend riding without underwear, saying it can cause chafing, itching, or even a rash. In the interest of research, I've ridden both ways, with and without underwear, and haven't seen much difference. If I were cycling long distances and having trouble with chafing, I'd drop the underwear in a flash. But, though I've worn bike shorts from a variety of manufacturers, I've never had even the hint of a rash. Do what works best for you.

Padded Gloves

A bicyclist's hands, wrists, and arms absorb an incredible amount of vibration, especially on bouncy backroads. Padded gloves will absorb it for you. And there's one other advantage to wearing gloves. When you take a fall, it's so much nicer to pick pointy stones out of padded gloves than out of your unpadded palms. You needn't worry about overheating; most bike gloves have open fingers and sweatproof backs, although fingered gloves are available for cool weather cycling. Padded gloves cost $15 to $30.

Sunglasses

When you're buying sunglasses, my advice is, don't buy glass. Plastic may not be as scratchproof, but if your head and the road ever make direct contact, you don't want glass between them. And though the ads in bike mags try to convince you otherwise, you don't need $200 wrap-arounds. Though they are better for eye-drying, high-speed, extralong downhill runs, cheap models will do fine for almost everything else. Nearly all sunglasses these days come with UV protection. Get ones that fit well, don't look entirely dorky, and are big enough to keep a mosquito from flying into your eye while you're doing 35 miles per hour.

To keep from scratching the lenses during cleaning, don't dry-wash them. Instead, rinse in lukewarm water, apply mild soap with your fingers, and dry with an optical cloth. Avoid rough cloths, paper towels, terry towels, or Kleenex. That way they'll last until the first time you sit on them. You can prevent that by attaching cords to the stems and wearing them around your neck.

Water Carrier

Cycling is dehydrating. Unlike tennis or racquetball, where you can feel the sweat dripping from your body, on a fast-moving bike, the wind dries the sweat as quickly as it forms. This cools your body, which is nice, but it also can fool you into thinking you're not losing fluids, which can be disastrous. When you bike, you need to drink. Which means you need to haul water. You have two options: a bottle and cage, which is attached to the bike frame, or a backpack hydration system.

Bottle and Cage. The bottle-and-cage system is lightweight and keeps the weight low on the bike. On the downside, although you can fit two or even three bottles on some bikes, you're carrying a limited amount of water. It's also a tad inconvenient to have to reach way down every time you want a drink and every time you replace the bottle. Some purists object to having holes drilled in their bike frames, though I've never seen or heard of any resulting damage.

Backpack Hydration System. Made popular by Camelbak, the backpack hydrator is composed of a plastic bladder, a soft pack to carry it, and a plastic tube to drink from. It holds a lot more water than a bottle and is more convenient to use. An added safety feature is that you don't have to take your hands or eyes off the road to get a drink. On the downside, you're carrying the weight high on your back instead of low and stable on your bike; the bladder requires cleaning and maintenance; and the price is about ten times that of the bottle and cage.

After years of drinking from a bottle, I finally tested two hydration systems, the Hydra Extreme and the Spinal Tap, both made by Quest. The former is a full-on backpack, the latter a mini-daypack. Both have a Platypus plastic reservoir inside. What I discovered was this: The water didn't have a plastic taste, the pack was comfortable on both smooth pavement and rocky roads, and drinking from a tube was much more convenient than reaching for my water bottle. In fact, it was so much more convenient, I ended up drinking at least half again as much as I normally would. This is a big plus; abundant water is a critical factor in completing a long ride without a major headache.

A word of caution. Whether you use a bottle or a hydration system, fill it only with clear, pure water. Lemonade may taste great, power drinks may—*may*—make you feel great, but anything other than water will begin the inevitable buildup of microbes and fungi. Soon you'll be bleaching your drinking vessel, and in a remarkably short time, you could be throwing it away.

Helmet

A helmet is the most important cycling accessory you can own and the best $30 to $150 you can spend. Helmets reduce the risk of serious head injury by 85 percent. And accidents happen. In 1997, more than 13,000 bicyclists were injured in California alone; 115 of them died. In Great Britain, around 25,000 accidents a year are serious enough to be reported to the Department of Transportation, and nearly 4,000 of them result in serious injury or death. In the United States, some 800 per year die in bike accidents, the vast majority having suffered a head injury. So get a helmet. Not a football helmet, not a used helmet—a new and unused bike helmet. In the past, you had to check the helmet's label to make sure it complied

with ANSI, ASTM, or Snell performance standards. But if your new helmet was made after March 10, 1999, it must by law meet the U.S. Con-
sumer Product Safety Commission standard.

Make sure the helmet fits snugly. Slip it on so it rests about one or two
finger widths above your eyebrows. If it feels loose, stick in the foam pads
that came with it. Now adjust the chinstrap until it's snug, too. The front
and back straps should meet just under your ears, and both should be
taut. Make sure the straps are easily adjustable.

When shopping for a helmet, look for comfort, lightness, and lots of
air vents so that your head will stay cool. If the helmet isn't cool and comfortable, you'll find reasons not to wear it. Coolness is an important safety
feature on long summer rides. That's why I believe that unless you live in
Alaska or the Yukon, the more vents, the better. But there is a trade-off: A
helmet with a lot of vents requires a harder foam that can put more load
on one small point of the skull.

Whatever helmet you buy, wear it. From time to time, check the fit and
readjust. Should you crash while wearing your helmet, thank it for saving
your brains, then throw it away. Bike helmets are made to save your IQ
only once.

Get your kids helmets, too. When fitting your child, don't do it just
before a ride. The process can take up to half an hour. Do it while he or she
is engaged in a book or listening to the radio.

•FAQ• **I wear padded pants and bike gloves, but I still hurt. What
should I do?**
The two parts of you that will suffer most when you cycle are your neck-
shoulder region and your bottom. To ease the strain, change position a lot.
Move your hands around on the handlebars, and stand up on your pedals.
If you get off your seat every ten minutes or so, you'll feel considerably
better at the end of the ride.

If your bottom still hurts, consider this suggestion from John Schubert,
technical editor of *Adventure Cyclist* magazine:

"My favorite mountain bike accessory is one of the oldest. In the early
1980s, Marin County frame builder Joe Breeze put into production an odd-
looking accessory called the Hite Rite. It's a spring that attaches to your
seatpost and allows you to raise and lower the seat while riding.

Opposite: **It looks a little odd, but a hydration system
is the best way to avoid dehydrating on long rides.**

"On steep descents, a rider wants to lower his body and put it rear-ward. This leads to an undignified-looking rider position, with the butt thrust out over the back wheel, but it allows you to safely control the bike under conditions that would leave other riders in dire risk of a pitchover accident. You can't attain this rider position very well without lowering your seat, and to do that, most people stop, get off the bike, and adjust the seat height.

"But with a Hite Rite, you simply flip open your seatpost quick release and put your weight on the saddle. The spring compresses, the seat lowers 2^1/$_2$ inches, and then you retighten the quick release. When you reach the bottom of the hill, you stand on the pedals, flip open the quick release, and the seat springs into optimum position for pedaling. You tighten the quick release, and you're done in less than five seconds, all without missing a pedal stroke." ■

High-End Cycling

N
W ◆ E
S

Just as with cross-country skiing, there's a major misconception about mountain biking. Both are seen as brown-bag sports, but in reality, North America is dotted with high-end resorts where mountain biking fits very comfortably with dinner jackets and an air of elegance.

Take the Balsams Grand Resort Hotel, for instance. High in Dixville Notch, New Hampshire's northernmost mountain pass, it has been serving well-heeled guests since 1853. It has all the expected amenities: fabulous dining room, perfect tennis courts, two manicured golf courses.

It also has 50 kilometers of delightfully nasty bike trails. In one afternoon, I rode over paved and unpaved road, grass and gravel, mud and rock, wet and dry surfaces. With a group of other guests, and led by the resort's mountain bike director, David Nesbitt, I circled lakes, paralleled streams, and watched for moose, bear, deer, and birds. I had a great time riding single track, double track, and maintenance road; climbing short, steep pitches; swooping down embankments; and stopping to take in scenic wonders.

Biking by the Balsams. Things could be worse.

Two hours later, I donned jacket and tie to sit down for a multicourse, multiforked dinner and would have gone dancing afterwards if all that mountain biking hadn't sapped my strength and sent me to bed early.

Best of all, the next morning I went out riding again, this time on entirely different trails. If I'd stayed a week, I think I could have found new places to ride every day. ▪

CHAPTER 4

Riding Paved Roads

As most of us live in highly paved areas, the vast majority of mountain bike owners spend much of their riding time on pavement. We need to ride the roads to get to the trails, and a lot of the backroads are paved.

John Schubert, a member of the board of directors of the League of American Bicyclists, author of two cycling books, and a technical editor who has published articles about cycling for over a quarter century, has this to say about road riding:

"Mountain bike riders shouldn't forsake the roads.

"In the years before the mid-1980s, an aspiring bike rider was likely to learn road skills. He learned to draft [discussed below] and be drafted in a tight pack of riders, to interact intelligently with traffic, and to behave like someone who belonged on the road.

"Today's mountain bike culture doesn't teach that. Some of the top mountain bike athletes can't draft worth beans and can't execute a proper left turn on the road. That's a shame, because we all should be in the business of learning as many cycling skills as possible. Just as road riders need to learn to jump obstacles and handle slippery surfaces (skills that are mostly the province of mountain bike riders), mountain bike riders really ought to learn road skills.

"Among mountain bike riders, I'm starting to hear some disturbing myths—that roads are unduly hazardous, that normal traffic is somehow more scary than it used to be, that bicyclists always need trails to ride. Bicycling is a lot less fun if you believe this nonsense.

"So learn to be a good road rider too. Pick up a road-riding book, join a local road-oriented cycling club, join the League of American Bicyclists and take one of its Effective Cycling courses.

"I enjoy both mountain trails and roads, and perhaps most importantly, I enjoy having developed the skills that go with both of these riding disciplines. Each makes you better at doing the other. So learn both and be a better rider in all ways."

The secret to long-distance highway biking is "steady does it." Bursts of frantic pedaling followed by long rests waste energy. Try to keep your pedals—not your tires—going at about the same pace on most terrain. A good cadence, the speed at which your pedals revolve, is 80 to 90 revolutions per minute.

Another steadiness factor is braking. Most cyclists do too much of it. As you gain confidence, practice *not* using your brakes on the long downhill runs. Bikes are pretty stable vehicles, particularly at high speeds.

There are three secrets to road biking that are so well known they've almost lost their secret status. They're the *before* secrets. One: Drink before you're thirsty. Two: Eat before you're hungry. Three: Shift before you need to. The drinking and eating are to save you from suddenly running out of energy, a condition known in biking circles as bonking, or hitting the wall. The shift is to spare you the indignity of trying to jam your way into low

Lake Groton. Paved roads can be backroads. (This isn't the Jersey Turnpike.)

gear while struggling up a hill. Gearing systems have greatly improved, but you do them no good by downshifting during the strain of a serious climb. Shift early, and if you miss the moment, circle around and shift during that downhill moment.

DRAFTING

A big part of the attraction of bicycling, as well as sports like skiing, roller skating, and ice skating, is getting something for nothing. By using gravity in skiing, momentum in skating, and gear ratios in bicycling, a modest output of energy moves you faster and farther than it would if you weren't on skis, skates, or wheels. It's that downhill swoop, that smooth glide over ice, that long roll after mashing down the pedal that give these sports their special thrill.

For bicyclists, there's another kind of free ride, one well known to racers and long-distance cyclists. It's called drafting.

Depending on conditions, drafting gives you up to a third more distance and speed with no extra expenditure of energy. It's like having an extra top gear on your car, a kind of superoverdrive.

What is drafting? Think of videos you've seen of a bicycle team racing down the road in single file, wheels almost touching. They're in a paceline, and they're drafting. The lead rider is doing most of the work. He's the one battling the wind, cutting an invisible but real swath through the air. The others are hitching a ride in his slipstream.

But you don't need to be an expert racer to draft. You don't need a team, either. Any two cyclists of moderate skill can do it. Here's how.

Drafting is legal.

Wear a helmet.

Start by practicing maintaining a steady pace over varying terrain. This is important to avoid collisions. Then, have one rider slip in behind the other. Because close drafting—poetically referred to in cycling circles as wheel sucking—is unnerving at first, the follower's front tire should be at least a yard behind the leader's rear tire. Work on that for a while, then slowly and gradually move in closer. You're aiming to get the tires within a foot of each other. That's when drafting approaches its maximum effectiveness.

Arrange a signal—say, "Hup!"—for the leader to announce an imminent gear change, and another signal—"Arrgggh!"—to announce imminent exhaustion. When that happens, the follower simply moves up and into the lead.

Once you're comfortable drafting with one other rider, invite other cyclists into the line. The longer the line, the less time each of you has to spend at the front.

Here are some drafting tips:

- Gradually force yourself to take your eyes off the leader's rear tire without losing track of where your front tire is in relation to hers. It can be done, and it reduces the mental strain by a large margin. It also lets you enjoy the scenery again.
- If you're uncomfortable directly behind the tire in front of you, move a few inches to either side. You'll still get most of the benefits of drafting.
- Don't overlap tires. That's just asking for trouble.
- Don't worry excessively about bumping tires. It's not a question of whether, it's a question of when. Since you know it will happen sometime, don't dwell on it. You don't fall in love every time you kiss, and you won't fall off your bike every time your tires kiss.
- If you find yourself heading for a tire kiss, let it happen. Don't try to avoid it with a last-second wheel turn. A tread-to-tread bump is a lot easier to recover from than a bump where one tire swerves sideways into another.
- When drafting, and when doing anything else on a bicycle, wear protective clothing, particularly a helmet.

Once you've more or less mastered all that, it's time to move into advanced drafting. Here's how it works. When a breeze is blowing, the wind direction determines where the sweet spot behind the lead rider falls. Adapt your riding position to the wind.

The maneuver is obviously not for use on a busy two-lane highway, but when your gang has the track to itself, it's cool to watch your buddies winging across the road like a flock of Canada geese. When the lead rider gives up the lead, she stays on the windward side, which gives the others a bit more wind shelter as she drops to the back of the pack.

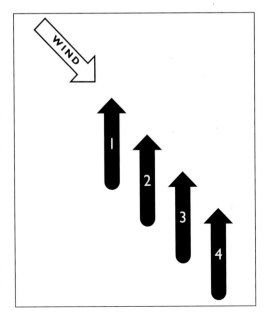

MASTERING GEARS

Here's the easy way to remember which gear to shift into: Front and rear, *the closer the chain is to the frame, the easier it will be to pedal.* The farther from the frame, the harder to pedal, but the farther you'll go each time you pedal.

When cyclists talk about gears, they generally refer to "high" or "low." Which is which? Here's how to remember: *High* is *hard. Low* is *languid.* When you're in high gear, you're working hard to push those pedals around. In low gear, the work is easier, but the pace is more languid.

By and large, you're better off in a lower gear. Spinning, when the pedals are turning fast and easy, takes much less effort in the long run than mashing the pedals. Most new cyclists do too much mashing and not nearly enough spinning.

How do you know you've chosen the right gear? Remember, the ideal cadence for paved road cycling is 80 to 90 pedal revolutions per minute. To figure that out, count the times your feet go around in ten seconds, then multiply by six. If that's too tedious, don't worry. Over time you get the feel for the cadence that works best for you.

HANDLING SHORT HILLS

You're riding along a road with lots of short, sharp hills. You come to a brief downhill followed by a short but steep uphill. And you have the feeling from the terrain that this won't be the last dip and climb you'll see today. What's the best way to handle it?

My advice is to blast down the first hill, stay in high gear at the bottom, and use the momentum to take you over the top of the rise. Not only is it fast and efficient, it's much more fun than shifting into low and crawling up the other side.

Paved Mountain Bike Treks

Sure, mountain bikes are rugged, versatile, and can go places, such as up mountains, that no bike has ever gone before. But the vast majority of people who buy mountain bikes don't ride up mountains. Instead, they ride on bike paths, sidewalks, paved roads, and other smooth, relatively level surfaces.

Let's look at three awesome-sounding but mostly downhill paved mountain bike treks.

One of the most ruggedly scenic spots east of the Rockies is Franconia Notch, New Hampshire's most famous mountain gap. To get there, take I-93 and get off at Exit 32. Drive 3 miles east to Loon Mountain, a major New Hampshire ski resort. Give the man a small amount of cash, and at 9 A.M., 11 A.M., 1:30 P.M., or 3:30 P.M., you and your bike (or *their* bike, for a little more cash) board a bus and ride to the top of the Notch and the beginning of the Franconia Notch Bicycle Path.

This is not your average bike path. It's perfectly paved, crosses gracefully arched bridges, and provides turnoffs complete with picnic tables. (Loon will provide you with a boxed lunch for a bit more cash.) The Franconia Notch Bicycle Path also has the advantage of running about 80 percent downhill, and most of its short uphill spurts are gentle.

Along the 8-mile path, you'll pass some of the state's premiere attractions: Echo Lake Beach, the Cannon Mountain Tram, and New Hampshire's best-known scenic gorge, the Flume. You can buy a combo ticket to all three for $10. For another dollar, you can visit the Ski Museum, which, is right beside the path.

It's 8 miles from the bike path's beginning at Echo Lake to its end at the Flume. You then pedal another 5 miles, about 3 of which are downhill, back to Loon and your car.

On the way, you'll pass famous New Hampshire tourist shrines: the Hobo Railroad; Whale's Tail Waterpark; Clark's Trading Post, complete with trained bears; and 273 factory outlet stores.

Across the Connecticut River in Vermont are other routes that are just as impressive-sounding and blessedly free of factory outlets. One is the Hazen's Notch road, which sounds bold enough, but you'll sound even tougher if you say, "I gave the old mountain bike a workout on the Bayley-Hazen Military Road."

You won't be lying. The Bayley-Hazen, approved by George Washington and paid for by the Continental Congress, was a road laid through the wilds of northern Vermont in 1776. It was meant to be a dagger aimed at the heart of British Canada. But it was a double-ended blade. The Brits simply waited for our side to finish construction, then strolled down the road and attacked *us*.

Today, mountain bikers can cruise down the same road. If you leave one car in the town of Lowell (just off Route 100) and drive west another 5 miles along Route 58 to the top of the Notch (marked by a plaque), you

can look forward to a sweet, fast ride along one of Vermont's most beautiful dirt roads—and it's *all downhill.*

This is the Vermont of your dreams. An impressive notch guarded by mountain sentinels. Ravens soaring in the blue sky. A nearly traffic-free road dappled with overhanging fir and maple. A gurgling stream. Even a campsite at the Hazen's Notch Campground.

The next trip is still farther north and sounds even more daring. Jay Peak is Vermont's northernmost ski mountain. It has a 4,000-foot summit, a 2,153-foot vertical drop, and 50 miles of skiable terrain. It also has the only aerial tramway in the state. And it's open to mountain bikers, who can take the tram up Jay Peak and bike down.

Although you never have to pedal, your forearms get a formidable workout as you white-knuckle the brakes, trying to keep within the speed of sound. Some of Jay's near-vertical black diamond trails are also open to cyclists, and these, it must be said, are not for the faint at heart. ▪

Opposite: **Jay Peak. Note the mechanical mode of ascendance at upper left.**

CHAPTER 5

Riding Dirt Roads

Now we're off the highway and we're really having fun. No more logging trucks, oil tankers, SUV-driving asphalt warriors, or asphalt. The noise, the congestion, the dangers of the highway are behind you now.

But leave one danger, and a new danger takes its place. The hidden danger of the dirt road is not the occasional rock, not the sporadic puddle, or even the unexpected ribbon of sand. No, the hidden danger of the dirt road is the town road crew. These folks are paid to hone the road, something they do once or twice a year. Honing removes those rocks, fills those

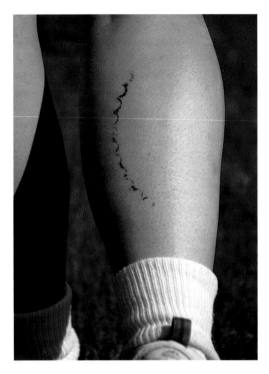

A chainring tatoo.

puddles, dissipates that sand. It keeps the road in great condition for driving. But it puts it in terrible condition for cycling. A hard-packed surface, even with occasional obstacles, is ideal for backroad biking. But honing covers that surface with a light layer of loose gravel, coarse sand, and dust, a nightmare coating for those who transport themselves on two wheels. A freshly honed road gives you no grip, no purchase, no feeling that the earth is firm beneath your feet. You slew and spin and curse the town road crew.

The solution? Take alternative routes until enough heavier vehicles have passed to restore a semblance of the old surface. If that's not practical, keep up a steady pace. Avoid sudden turns and bursts of power. And be ready to dismount at a moment's notice.

Another problem is that your chain seems much more likely to come off the chain ring on a dirt road than on a paved highway. It's a moment of deep despair, for you know that your rhythm is about to be broken, your ride interrupted, your hands blackened with dirty chain grease.

Unless you know this trick: When your chain jumps off the ring, *keep on pedaling!* You stand a fair chance of getting it to jump back on all by itself. You stand an even better chance if you shift as though you were changing gears.

Since the alternative is stopping, dismounting, pulling the nasty thing back on the sprocket with grease-encrusted fingers, trying to wipe your hands on what turns out to be poison ivy, and using strong language in front of the children, this is a tip to treasure forever.

HORSES

It's on dirt roads that you're most likely to encounter horses. Horses, which appear totally unfazed by passing cars and trucks, are easily spooked by bikes. A spooked horse is a dangerous animal, especially to the person sitting on its back. Here's how to avoid creating a scary situation.

If you see a horse and rider coming your way, dismount and stay dismounted until they pass. If you come upon them from behind, dismount, then call out to the rider, letting her know you're there. Either way, pass the horse on foot. Just why this is so much less frightening than if you were on the bike is anyone's guess, but trust me, it is.

DOGS

The barking, bounding, potentially attacking dog is the cyclist's nightmare, and they're most commonly found lying in wait beside backroads. What do you do when man's best friend comes after you?

The very best thing you can do is to make the dog *your* best friend. Slow down. Say, "Nice doggy." Carry dog treats and hand them out generously. Pet the dog if it seems friendly enough.

Sometimes this doesn't work. When you sense you are about to be savaged, move swiftly into plan B. Plan B is to make the dog afraid of you, more afraid than you are of it, if that's possible. Forget the treats. Throw pebbles, then rocks, then spears—anything but using Mace.

While a canister of Mace is good for revenge fantasies, it's not much use in the saddle. It's just too hard to aim a vapor stream when being chased by a fanged and foaming cur. A handful of stones is more accurate and better at getting instant attention. If you don't have stones, give him a squirt from your water bottle. Using a hydration system? Take a big mouthful and spit.

When you run out of ammunition, go to plan C. Steer your bike directly at the snarling dog. Make eye contact. Look extremely serious. Say, *"Revennnggge!"* Most dogs will run when confronted with a bike bearing down on them, powered by an insane person.

But if this, too, fails, move into plan D. Get off the bike and place it between you and dog. Use it as a shield as you call for help or back away.

DEER AND MOOSE

Deer? Oh, yes. And moose, too. Pedaling down a steep Vermont dirt road early one morning, Effin and I encountered a moose in the middle of the road. If you see a moose, dismount. Keep your distance. Under no circumstances try to ride around him. The way he sees it, you're on his piece of road. You try to pass at your own considerable risk.

As for deer, one of Vermont's best cyclists hit or was hit by a deer while descending a steep road at 40 miles an hour. The deer appeared surprised but had the wherewithal to kick the cyclist in the back before bounding into the woods. The cyclist spent the next four weeks recuperating from bruises and poison ivy. His bike was destroyed.

Hey, it's a jungle out there. But don't forget to taste the berries!

ADVANTAGES OF BACKROAD RIKING

If you told me that for the rest of my life, I could only ride one surface—highway, unpaved backroad, or offroad woods trails—I'd be extremely unhappy. I love the mix that biking offers, and I'd vigorously protest any limitations on my ability to enjoy them all.

But if my hand were forced, I'd choose backroad bicycling. In fact, most of my riding time is spent on unpaved lanes. Some are well-traveled dirt roads, some graveled rails-to-trails paths, some semiabandoned, partially washed-out byways running from nowhere to nowhere.

What's the appeal? Well, the view, for one. I can see for a mile from a high dirt road, 50 yards from a woodsy trail, the back of the truck in front of me from the highway. Safety (or at least what I perceive as safety) is another. I'd much rather take my chances with a farm dog than an eighteen-wheeler, and I like not wondering if I'm about to fall off a cliff around every blind corner in the forest.

But there are a couple of other things as well. One is companionship. I can bike beside my wife and friends much more easily on a backroad than on a single-track trail or a busy freeway. One of my neighbors who sometimes rides with us complains that I'm always stopping for a chat. It's true, and for me, it's another backroad pleasure. And finally, because I'm naturally nosy, I like the chance to look in on local civilization. Peering at the mansions in Palm Beach, at a lighthouse on Prince Edward Island, at my neighbors on their front porch in Vermont—these are the pleasures of the backroad. For me, this is smelling the honeysuckle.

•FAQ• I have an old, preindex shifting bike, and sometimes after a shift, I can hear that the gears need tickling, either in the front or the rear. How do I tell which lever to play with?
You can tell whether it's the front or rear gear that needs adjusting by the sound. Keep listening to your gears, and before long you'll be able to get it right nine times out of ten. ■

Opposite: **Tasting the berries.**

The Bay of Fundy Trail

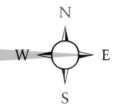

Fundy Trail Parkway is the newest addition to New Brunswick's provincial tourism infrastructure. It's a winding road along the cliffs that line the Bay of Fundy. Beside the parkway, and even closer to the cliffs, is the Fundy Trail, a multiuse path for cycling and hiking.

I did both, but not by design. I'd intended to bike, and I must say I may have sneered when park interpreter Wanda Ellis said, "You can bike the whole 11 kilometers if you like." "If you like" meaning "if you can."

Somehow, I didn't think that would be a problem. I'd just come from mountain biking much longer mileage than that in the mountains of Vermont, and I sure didn't see any mountains around here.

So imagine my surprise when, halfway up the first hill, I found myself walking. Pushing my bike. Sweating and muttering like a fool. And eating my sneer.

The start of the Fundy Trail is steep. I thought it defined steep. It's steeper than just about anything I ever rode in Vermont. It's steep enough that I dismounted more than once, concerned lest I suffer cardiac arrest in a maritime province. But once I'd rested and recovered, I have to say, it's about the best laid-out bike trail I've ever ridden.

The Fundy Trail is about 90 percent packed gravel, but when the going gets steep, it's paved to facilitate climbing and, more important, to prevent erosion. The trail passes through dappled woods, across sturdy wooden bridges, up and down copses, hills, mounds, hummocks, dips, valleys, and hollows. It's all-terrain heaven.

But what sets this trail apart is not the surface or the terrain, but the neighborhood. The trail does its winding and climbing and dipping atop the cliffs beside the Bay of Fundy. With its 40- to 50-foot tides, the bay is an official Natural Wonder of the World. But more important, it's a scenic wonder of the world. The water is all that blue can be. The cliffs drop onto broad, graveled beaches. On the horizon, the coast of Nova Scotia drowses under lazy clouds. The scent of balsam fills the air, and the loudest sound is the squawk of seabirds.

As if that weren't enough, picnic tables, litter bins, and even water fountains are strategically placed in the most scenic spots. In terms of location, design, and amenities, this is one bike path that's been well thought out.

Even if it did turn me into a walker. ■

CHAPTER 6

Riding Offroad

There's nothing like offroad cycling. If getting off the highways and onto dirt roads means shedding oil tankers and road-raged commuters, getting off dirt roads and into the woods means shedding the motorcycles, pickup trucks, and yahoos cruising in fat-tired cars with their windows open and sharing the blast of their stereos with the rest of the world. Here in the woods, it's just you, the birds, and the trees.

Not long ago, Effin and I were taking a San Francisco couple on a tour of Albany. Riding down Water Street (the only street in Albany, Vermont, other than Old Street and New Street), we enjoyed the timeless, simple country pleasure of making city folks look foolish. As they oohed and ahh-hed about the deer standing stock still in a field, we chuckled. Sure enough, it wasn't long before they discovered it was standing still because it wasn't a deer but a deer target, put there to give the homeowner practice before bow season.

Then we pedaled up the hill, past Page Pond, and ducked into a pasture. Following the twin ruts of a hay-wagon path, we nearly fell off our bikes when a couple of *real* deer bounded by, not 50 yards away.

And that's the difference between backroad and offroad.

But when you enjoy the pleasures of the wild, you take on the risks of the wild. These include getting lost, getting cold, getting hungry and thirsty, and, in certain parts of Montana and California, getting eaten by a grizzly bear or mountain lion. Becoming a carnivore's lunch isn't all that likely, but the other risks are real concerns. It behooves you to be prepared. Here are some tips from biker Lennard Zinn:

- Always take plenty of water.
- Tell someone where you are going and when you expect to return.

- Take matches, extra clothing and food, and perhaps a flashlight and an aluminized emergency blanket.
- If the area is new to you, go with someone who is familiar with it, or take a map and compass, and know how to use them.
- Wear a helmet.
- Take a basic first aid kit and bike tools. Know how to use them.
- If you find personal effects on the ground, assume they could indicate that someone is lost or in trouble. Report the find and mark the location.
- If you get lost, backtrack.
- Don't go down something you can't get back up.
- Walk your bike when it's appropriate. Falling off a cliff is a poor alternative to taking a few extra seconds or displaying less bravado.
- Don't ride beyond your limits. Take a break. Get out of the hot sun. Avoid dehydration and bonk by eating and drinking enough.
- Teach your friends all these things.

GENERAL ADVICE

Listening to offroaders talk, the words you'll hear most often are single track and double track. Single track generally means a trail just wide enough for one bike at a time; double track allows for side-by-side riding. About double track, one wise mountain biker gave me this bit of wisdom: "No matter which track you choose, the other one's gonna be better."

My own single best piece of advice for dirt and dirt roads is this: Ride it out. When you're struggling up a boulder-strewn track and you feel you can't crank out one more turn of the pedals, take a deep breath and keep going till you ride it out. When you're tearing down a fire road and swerving from side to side in an endless rut, don't dismount—ride it out. When you're halfway through an endless swamp of chain-sucking mud, ride it out. You'll be amazed at how much farther you can go than you thought you could.

And here's my second-best advice: When you're bouncing down a hill, try to keep your upper body relaxed. That "quiet upper body" is nearly as important in mountain biking as it is in alpine skiing and other lower-body sports.

If you're using toeclips or clipless pedals, you can use the entire pedal stroke for power. Here's what I mean. The way you learned to bike was to push down on the pedal to induce forward motion. Pedaling round means pressuring not only the downstroke, but the upstroke as well. In fact, pedaling round means pressuring the entire range of pedal motion: the downstroke, as the pedal pushes to the rear, on the upstroke, and when it's driving forward getting ready for the next downstroke.

Why bother learning this new technique when the old one got you through your entire childhood cycling career? Because pedaling round is much more efficient. It gives you extra power instantly. It uses and exercises all your leg muscles. It's better.

For some, it helps to concentrate on three points of the stroke. Focus on *pedaling back* at the bottom, *lifting* on the backstroke, and *driving* toward the handlebars at the end of the stroke.

Here are some additional offroad riding tips from Bruce Spicer, a leading World Cup racer, Canadian national title holder, resident test pilot for Brodie Bikes, and head instructor at Velo-City, a Vancouver bike expedition company.

- The front brake is your friend.

  Don't believe people who tell you to ignore the front brake because it will fling you over the bars. Use a smooth, steady squeeze on the brake lever, and you'll soon learn to brake hard without flipping or

skidding. You'll have more control over your stopping ability, and
the trails will thank you.
- Where you look is where you go.
  When choosing a line through the terrain, look up the trail at where
  you want to end up, not where you don't. Following your eyes will
  guide you away from obstacles.
- Ride the bike, don't let it ride you.
  Suspension developments are taking away the need to use body
  English more and more. But to really ride a bike well, you still need
  to help it over even the smallest obstacles, as well as into dips and
  holes in the trail. Your hands control the front wheel, your feet control the rear.
- Be prepared.
  Pumps, spares, and a change of clothes can make a world of difference to your ride. Splitting the responsibilities on longer trips makes
  sense—one rider brings a chain break, another brings a spare derailleur, and so on. Everybody should bring spare tubes, though.

TURNING ON DIRT

If you've driven your car over icy roads, you've probably already learned
to brake before you turn. It's the same on a bike—to avoid the kind of skid
that leads directly to the ditch, brake before you turn. The laws of motion,
gravity, and the universe don't allow you to do both at the same time and
get away with it.

Also as when driving a car, you can decrease the tightness of a turn by
using the whole road. Even on a single track, the path is much wider than
your tires. Use as much of it as you can, swinging wide before the turn so
you don't end up scraping the side of the trail.

Here's advanced advice from one of the world's greatest mountain
bikers, Ned Overend:

"Press your outside foot against the pedal at the bottom of the stroke
to force the bike into the ground. With all your weight on your outside
foot, you can do a tighter turn at a higher speed. Your hips should tilt with
the bike to the inside of the turn, but your shoulders should remain over
your outside foot. Focus all of your weight on the outside pedal. This
keeps more weight over the tires, pushing the knobs into the dirt while
still letting the bike carve.

OPPOSITE: **Ride it out!**

R U L E S O F T H E T R A I L

Thousands of miles of dirt trails have been closed to mountain bicyclists. The irresponsible riding habits of a few riders have been a factor. Do your part to maintain trail access by observing the following rules of the trail, formulated by the International Mountain Bicycling Association (IMBA). IMBA's mission is to promote environmentally sound and socially responsible mountain bicycling.

1. Ride on open trails only.

Respect trail and road closures (ask if not sure), avoid possible trespass on private land, obtain permits or other authorization as may be required. Federal and state wilderness areas are closed to cycling. The way you ride will influence trail management decisions and policies.

2. Leave no trace.

Be sensitive to the dirt beneath you. Even on open (legal) trails, you should not ride under conditions where you will leave evidence of your passing, such as on certain soils after a rain. Recognize different types of soils and trail construction; practice low-impact cycling. This also means staying on existing trails and not creating new ones. Don't cut switchbacks. Be sure to pack out at least as much as you pack in.

3. Control your bicycle!

Inattention for even a second can cause problems. Obey all bicycle speed regulations and recommendations.

4. Always yield trail.

Make known your approach well in advance. A friendly greeting or bell is considerate and works well; don't startle others. Show your respect when passing by slowing to a walking pace or even stopping. Anticipate other trail users around corners or in blind spots.

5. Never spook animals.

All animals are startled by an unannounced approach, a sudden movement, or a loud noise. This can be dangerous for you, others, and the animals. Give animals extra room and time to adjust to you. When passing horses, use special care and follow directions from the horseback riders (ask if uncertain). Running cattle and disturbing wildlife are serious offenses. Leave gates as you found them, or as marked.

6. Plan ahead.

Know your equipment, your ability, and the area in which you are riding—and prepare accordingly. Be self-sufficient at all times, keep your equipment in good repair, and carry necessary supplies for changes in weather or other conditions. A well-executed trip is a satisfaction to you and not a burden or offense to others. Always wear a helmet and appropriate safety gear.

Keep trails open by setting a good example of environmentally sound and socially responsible offroad cycling.

"Making a successful turn depends on finding the balance between leaning the bike over and keeping enough weight on the tires to keep them from sliding out. You might want your weight slightly heavy on the front to facilitate turning traction."

Note in the photo of mountain bike racer Jesse Terhune coming around a corner at speed how he uses the bike's lean, not the handlebars, to make the turn. Except at low speed, leaning, not pivoting, is the way to go. Note, too, that his weight is centered between the handlebars and the seat, and that his butt is off the seat. This puts enough weight on the front tire to keep it in firm contact with the ground. The back wheel can slide a bit without tossing you, but the front must be rock solid.

Former racer John Schubert thinks that one of the most important skills is instant turning. Schubert points out that the technique requires skill and a lot of practice. Here's John Schubert on the instant turn:

"Initiate the turn with a quick and large movement of the handlebars in the wrong direction. In a tenth of a second, your bike is about one foot

Jesse leans into a turn.

off to one side of you. Now you whip the handlebars in the other direction. With your body off to one side like that, you instantly begin a sharp turn, with the bike leaned far over."

CLIMBING HILLS

Greg Danford is a freelance copywriter and outdoor specialist living in Woodstock, Vermont. He's also a total mountain bike fanatic. Here's his advice on climbing:

"Try not to stand up in the saddle, as it removes weight from your rear wheel, reducing traction. Also, try to keep your forearms parallel to your bike's top tube (the one that runs underneath your crotch). This will keep your front wheel from popping up. If you must stand, keep your hips over the rear wheel. This will prevent you from spinning out."

Try not to shift down on the front derailleur while you're climbing a steep hill. Overloading the ring can lead to chain suck, meaning that the chain gets stuck in the ring and won't let go. Since chain suck happens suddenly, this can lead to an out-of-bicycle experience in which you see yourself rising above the handlebars and hurtling toward a waiting oak tree.

Avoid this by shifting down on the rear derailleur instead of the front one and by shifting before you hit the steepest part of the hill. If this doesn't work, speed up, then coast and shift while you're coasting. If none of this works, turn around and make a tight circle, shifting on the downhill before resuming your climb.

Here's another tip from champion rider Ned Overend:

"To climb most effectively, concentrate on mastering smooth transitions between a range of sitting and crouched standing positions.

"By moving around your weight, which is centered near your hips, you can maximize traction. Your body position constantly adjusts to maintain purchase with the rear wheel and steering control with the front wheel.

"When climbing in the saddle, it's a balancing act between traction and steering. If the front end is light, bend at the waist and lower your chest toward the handlebars. You can also weight the front end more by sliding forward on the saddle. Using a combination of these two movements keeps enough weight over the rear wheel without losing control of the front.

"A common error is shifting to the little chain ring too soon when approaching a hill climb. This can cause a loss of momentum at the base of a climb, where it's needed the most. Instead, shift progressively, running through the gears one or two at a time. We have twenty-four gears—use them!"

The photo below illustrates the right way to climb a steep hill. The rider's butt is far enough back to keep the traction on the rear wheel. He's out of the saddle and on his feet for powerful pedaling. And he's using his arms to add power to his pedaling.

In the next photo, the rider is ascending the wrong way. He's so far forward his rear tire is likely to start slipping. When that happens, he'll lose the precious momentum that will get him to the top.

The time will come when you meet a hill you cannot climb. It may be strewn with boulders or dripping with mud or steeper than a church door. Whatever the cause, a third of the way up, you suddenly realize you aren't going up anymore. Reluctantly, you dismount and start pushing. As you look up at the remainder of the hill, you realize it's going to be a long walk. Here's where this tip will help: Instead of pushing from the handlebars, *drop one hand back to the seat*. Now you're in a more comfortable position; pushing the bike to the top becomes considerably easier, if no more dignified.

Good climbing. The weight stays on the rear wheel for power.

Bad climbing Notice how far forward the butt is from the saddle.

RIDING DOWNHILL

The best position for cycling downhill, particularly down a bumpy, rutted hill, is up on the pedals, knees bent, elbows bent, and butt as far back as possible. The bike absorbs the punishment, and you enjoy the ride.

The trick to riding downhill is to resist natural tendencies. First, don't ride the brakes. When descending a long hill, especially one filled with rocks and roots, the natural tendency is to keep the brakes engaged. A better strategy is to use the brakes when you need them, but keep them fully released when you don't. It's easier on the brake pads, but more important, it's much easier on your forearm muscles. Let them relax between workouts—and that means hands off the brake levers.

When riding pell-mell down a rough road or track, resist the natural tendency to tighten your grip on the handlebars. Instead, loosen your grip.

OPPOSITE: Good pushing. One hand on the saddle, one on the bars.

The rougher the road, the looser your grip should become. On a really fast, bumpy descent, go one step further and let your hands ring the bars without touching. That way, two things happen. The tires find their own best track, and the bike absorbs the punishment, not your forearms. It's also good to get up out of the saddle. Pedal until your cranks are level, then rise up on them. Depending on how rough the track is, you may only need to straddle the saddle, or it may be best to get up high enough to clear it completely. Your sensitive body parts will thank you.

On fast downhills, I slip out of my toeclips or snap out of my clipless pedals. Other riders, such as expert cyclist David Porter, do the opposite, making sure they're firmly attached to their bikes. You'll know pretty quickly which camp you're in; if you feel safer with a bike solidly under you, stay clipped. If you feel like you're tied to a log racing over a waterfall, do the following: With toeclips, pull your feet free, raise them above the pedals, and the weight of the clips swivel the pedal upside-down. Then put your feet back on the pedal and keep going. With clipless pedals, snap out and keep your feet in a position that doesn't let them snap back in. In case of a sudden upending, this will prevent you from being locked onto the bike as it careens over a bank.

Let's look at what all this really means. At right, above, is David Nesbitt coming down a hill the right way. Notice that his arms are bent, he's sitting way back on the saddle, and his fingers are ready to brake if necessary.

The bottom photo shows Nesbitt coming down the wrong way. He's so far forward that if he hits a rock or hits the brakes, he could go flying over the handlebars.

When the going *really* gets steep, take this advice from Greg Danford: "Keep your weight as far back as possible. In very steep terrain, some experienced riders push their hips behind and below their seat. Although your front brake has far more stopping power, resist the temptation to use it by itself. You may find yourself in a situation where your bike stops and you keep going, resulting in a rather rude introduction to terra firma."

If the road is stony, deeply rutted, or mined with protruding roots, whenever you're not pedaling, bring your pedals parallel to the ground. It's not as relaxing a position riding at 3:00 or 9:00 as at 6:00 or 12:00, but it's a lot more relaxing than catching your 6:00 foot on a snag and ending up on the ground.

Here are some tips from biking legend Ned Overend on downhill riding: "Get your weight back as the grade gets steeper. Moving back and focusing your weight on your feet keeps your weight centered between

Good descending. The butt is behind the saddle.

Bad descending. That high and forward butt is an invitation to a fall.

the tires. This stance will give you confidence and stability. You won't get bounced around, and you'll be positioned to counteract braking forces and to unweight the front wheel so it can roll over obstacles.

"It sounds counterintuitive, but an important thing to remember on descents is to relax. Be fluid with your movements. If you're relaxed, with your knees and arms bent, you'll help the tires stay in contact with the ground for more controlled braking and cornering traction. Keep a firm grip with your hands, but make sure muscle tension does not extend up your arms. If your legs and arms are rigid, you'll transmit more shock up to the rest of your body. You can't think or see clearly if you are being rattled around."

Braking is at the heart of downhill biking. Here's John Schubert on braking.

"On a bike, the front brake has much more stopping power than the rear brake. But wanton, reckless use of the front brake can cause a pitchover accident. There is a time-honored technique by which a skilled

Bad braking has immediate and observable consequences.

rider can avoid pitchover accidents. Apply both brakes. Squeeze the front brake two or three times as hard as the rear brake. If the *rear* wheel skids, let up on the *front* brake.

OBSTACLES

For many new dirt riders, obstacles are intimidating. That's not surprising. But just as the city rider learns to avoid pedestrians, weave around parked vans, and dodge suddenly opening car doors, so does the dirt rider learn to handle protruding roots, thorny vines, and gurgling streams. In both cases, the defensive action begins with knowing how to look where you're going. Here's how veteran cyclist Greg Danford puts it:

"Look where you want to go, not where you're afraid to go. By glancing at a log or a rut that you want to avoid, you start a chain reaction that could lead to disaster. First your eyes move, then your head, and finally your shoulders and arms start steering you into the obstacle. Better to concentrate on where you're going."

But what if you come to a really big obstacle—say, a tree across the path? Now you're getting into the advanced stuff that separates the mountain biking backroads expert from the rest of the pack. Expert mountain biker Jesse Terhune shows two ways to get over a fallen tree.

The first is to *ride over it*. Balance in place just before running into the obstacle. Pop a small wheelie to place your front tire onto the log. Keep

Up one side . . .

pedals parallel . . .

. . . and down the other.

your pedals level when you're on the log. As soon as the front tire drops off the far side, heave your rear end up to lift the back of the bike onto the log. It helps if you lightly dab the front brake.

The other way over is considerably more spectacular. It's called the *bunny hop*. Get a fast start, and as you approach the log, crouch and spring. Use your whole body. As you spring, bring the bike with you—you're both airborne. Clear the obstacle in the air and ride off into the sunset. Two things help. Most such techniques, especially this one, are easiest with clip-in pedals, hardest with plain platform pedals. And, when attempting a bunny hop, your weight should be evenly distributed fore and aft and side to side. Your pedals should be even and parallel to the ground. You should take off from and try to land on both wheels.

MUD

Mud is to mountain biking as crud is to skiing, and seaweed is to sea kayaking. Sooner or later—probably sooner—you're going to have to deal

Bunny hopping: pedals even, wheels even, rider evenly balanced.

Opposite: **Too much aggression in mud . . .**

**. . . has immediate and
observable consequences.**

with it. With all three, you need a strong, steady, aggressive attack to get through it without becoming one with it. What you want to avoid is short, choppy pedal strokes; steady power is the key here, and the best way to maintain it is to *stay in the saddle*. Crossing a field of mud is not the time to get up on the pedals and jam. That's the best way to dig yourself in. Instead, keep your meat on the seat and keep up a steady cadence until you reach solid ground again. When you finally do, lunge forward to get your rear wheel free from the muck.

SAND

Sand sucks. No, that's not a pejorative, merely a statement of fact. When you're riding over (actually, through) sand, you feel your wheel being sucked to a standstill and your energy sucked out of your body. It's hard going.

But not impossible. These tricks should help. First, just as with mud, stay in the saddle. Once you stop in sand, you stop for good. But don't assume your usual seated position—get way back on the saddle to give yourself extra rear-wheel traction. If you're going downhill through sand, get even farther back to avoid achieving liftoff the first time you hit your front brakes. Use low gears. And when you need to turn, do it by leaning, not by turning the handlebars. Swiveling the front wheel while struggling to maintain forward motion is a quick way to eat sand.

DROP-OFFS

There's a moment of truth when you're offroad cycling. You come to a lip that drops off sharply—and calls invitingly for you to drop in. You can do it, if you know how.

Notice how far back Jesse is, below, and notice that he's so low that his stomach is actually resting on the seat. What you can't see is that before taking the plunge, he thoroughly checked the ground for loose rocks, stray branches, half-hidden holes—all the things that could change a landing from triumph to pratfall. You should do the same before heading down the steep.

TRICKS

You could argue that every trick you master makes you a better rider. That's true, of course. But the real reason to learn the tricks that follow is that you look cool when you're doing them. That, and the envy you create among trick-deprived friends.

For whatever reasons, if you're feeling bold or bored, try doing wheelies and wheel stands. To pop a wheelie, balance in place, then shift your weight forward, lock the brakes, and heave back until the front wheel rises. A rear wheel stand is the same thing, only holding the pose.

Saddle meets stomach for a successful drop-in.
OPPOSITE: Popping a wheelie.

A one-hand wheelie (top) and a no-hand wheelie.

A front wheel stand is just the opposite. It looks just like the picture of bad braking on page 78. Riding at low speed, lightly dab the front brake and shift your weight forward. Use your feet to raise the back of the bike. It's a lot easier if they're clipped in. Wave to the admiring onlookers. Next, work on your one-hand wheelie . . . and your no-hand wheelie.

FALLING

You will fall. Sooner or later, nearly all cyclists do. But 99 percent of the time, it's no big deal, as long as you know how to do it safely. This is the kind of thing to think about beforehand, to rehearse in your mind so that when the moment comes, you can do it automatically.

To avoid an incipient fall, *steer toward it*. This takes practice, but just as you steer into a skid in a car, steer into a fall on a bike. If you feel yourself falling to the left, steer left.

But if the fall can't be avoided, you can still minimize the damage. When you feel the fall coming, get out of your pedals. Leap clear of the bike. Aim, if you can, for soft ground. And when you land, try to *roll in the direction you're already moving*. Rounded shoulders are much better at dissipating the force of impact than your hands, wrists, or head. These are the body parts you don't want to land on.

Falling.

Rolling gets you away from the bike and protects your most breakable body parts.

If you feel a fall coming when you're barreling down a steep hill, there's an even better trick. Because your butt is already way back behind the seat, just let the bike go—assuming you've already removed your feet from the pedals, of course. With luck, you'll find yourself standing upright with the bike in front of you, rolling down the hill like a riderless horse.

•FAQ• Is it better to shift the rear or front gears?

It depends on what you're doing. According to David Porter, on rolling terrain, when you need a lower gear to make it over the next rise and you don't want to lose momentum, shift from the cogs in the back. But if you're facing a climb that's going to go on for a while, get into a smaller chain ring in front before mashing the pedals. If you find you're now in too low a gear, shift up in the back till the going gets tougher, then start downshifting in the back.

If you think of the front chain rings as different ranges and the cogs in back as choices within each range, your use of the gears will make a lot more sense. Better to think of your twenty-seven-speed bike as having three sets of nine rather than twenty-seven separate gears. ■

Opposite: **The view from the Seawall.**

Cycling Vancouver

More than any other city I know, Vancouver is an outdoor playground. Nowhere on the continent—if, indeed, the world—is so much outdoor adventure so close to the heart of an urban center of 2 million. Right in the heart of the city is Stanley Park, the largest urban park in North America, its 1,000 acres include rose gardens, giant Douglas firs, an ever-changing sidewalk art gallery, and a justly famous aquarium.

But best of all is what surrounds the park: 7 miles of walking, skating, and cycling path called the Seawall. It started as a make-work Depression project in 1929, and in some ways, it's been under construction ever since. For a reasonable sum, you can rent skates or, better, a bike nearby, and start your way around the Seawall.

You'll pass a cricket match, a game of bowls, a small forest of totem poles. You'll smell sea air and pine forest and the coconut scent of tanning oil. You'll hear the whistle of a freighter, the warning cry of a gull, the hum

of cars passing directly overhead on the Lions Gate Suspension Bridge. You'll see tall harbor cranes backed by much taller mountains, sun worshipers stretched out on beaches, giant trees growing so close to the path that you have to duck to get around them. By the end of the excursion, you'll know infinitely more about Vancouver than if you'd driven its crowded streets searching for a place to park.

For a very different kind of cycling less than a half hour from town, try Grouse Mountain. There are two ways to do it: from the bottom up or from the top down. For the latter, arrange with Velo City (www.velo-city.com) to pick you up and deliver you to the Grouse Mountain cable car. Electric power, not pedal power, takes you to 3,700 feet, where Velo City has a mountain bike and mountain guide awaiting your arrival.

You pedal down, always down, a steep and winding mountain road. Even in midsummer, you may pass by pockets of snow and feel the waves of cold as you cross a fast-flowing mountain stream. You cycle through high alpine meadows, across precipitous ski slopes, and through dark rain forests. Three or four hours later, you emerge in a suburban neighborhood, exhilarated, maybe exhausted, and ready to tumble into the van for a lift back to the hotel.

That's pedaling *down* Grouse. Pedaling up is another story. Though you start on the same mountain road, you're going slow enough to notice nearly invisible paths leading off to the left and right. Some are nothing more than 2-foot breaks in the trees, and none are marked with signs or arrows. Follow these trails to adventure.

They lead into what have been described as the hardest mountain bike trails in the world. In addition to the considerable natural obstacles—giant boulders, fallen trees, rushing streams—Vancouver's mountain bike fanatics have added impediments of their own. Like a foot-wide plank linking two boulders 15 or 20 feet apart. Being in a rain forest, the plank's surface is slippery, but to ensure you're sufficiently challenged, it's wedged in on a double sloping angle, 10 feet above the ground. And if you do manage to cross that long, narrow board, you still have to hop off the boulder and down to the ground.

Welcome to Vancouver, mountain biker. ■

CHAPTER 7

Family Biking

There are three things you should know about Le Tour de la Montagne Bromont, an annual bike event held a half hour or so east of Montreal in the Eastern Townships of Quebec. First, it will be the best organized bike event—maybe any event—you'll ever experience. The trails are marked, the porta-potties are clean, the hot dogs are tasty, and the only motorized vehicle you'll encounter in the afternoon's ride around the mountain is the circling Jeep whose driver ensures you have sufficient water to quench your thirst.

Second, the route covers nearly the full range of backroad biking: paved highway (though without cars), gravel roads, dirt roads, double track, single track, muddy spots, rutty spots, boulder-strewn spots, farm fields, streams, ups, downs, and levels. Yet not one bit of it is too hard for the novice cyclist to handle.

Third, the entire event, from the group calisthenics before the start, to the signs along the trail, to the helpful guides who stand at tricky corners telling you which way to go, is handled in French. The fifteen hundred cyclists around you are all speaking French. Yet if you ask a question in English, you'll get a cheerful reply in that language.

Isn't this what you spend big money to go to Europe for? And all too often don't find? The whole gestalt—the happy crowd, the beautiful organization, the variety of safe riding experiences, the exotic yet friendly culture—makes Le Tour an ideal place to bring your cycling family. Or introduce your family to cycling.

Whatever it is, Le Tour emphatically is not a race. Sure, the fast gang (mostly prepubescent boys) takes off first, but there's no prize for the fastest, no shame for the slowest. In many ways, Le Tour is the opposite of the corner mountain-bike manufacturers have worked themselves into in their pursuit of the speed-mad teenage male. There are plenty of teenagers

at Le Tour, but they're not leaping off cliffs. There are nearly as many females as males. There are toddlers, grandmothers, and every age in between. And while most of the bikes you see are mountain bikes, there are also plenty of hybrids.

I'm clearly a big fan of the Bromont event, but what I'd like even more is to see a hundred such events spring up all over North America. It's hard to imagine a better way to get families cycling together.

TANDEM RIDING

If you prefer cycling with just your honey (and maybe a baby), consider the tandem, popularly known as the bicycle built for two. Ben Hewitt, who writes about cycling, skiing, and country life for a variety of publications, captains a tandem. His wife, Penny Griggs, is the fearless stoker. Together they've covered many a backroad and even offroad mile on a tandem bike. If this appeals to you, here's Ben's expert advice:

> My wife and I have been riding a tandem bicycle offroad for over five years. We weren't married when we bought our tandem, and we take great pride in the fact that five years of bouncing through the woods on a bicycle built for two did not dissuade us from formalizing our union in 1998.
>
> Tandem mountain biking demands an intuitive level of communication that can be developed only with time in the saddle. The challenge is the relationship of the captain (forward position, typically occupied by the larger of the two) and stoker (rear position, requiring the utmost of faith in the captain) surviving this often rocky period intact.
>
> There are no secrets to successful offroad tandeming, but common sense and good manners do apply: common sense, in that it is important to realize the limitations of a tandem on tight mountain trails; good manners, in that it is crucial for the captain, who controls shifting, steering, and braking, to verbally warn the stoker before these actions are taken. Consider the laws of physics: Your tandem is almost 7 feet long from tread to tread, and combined with two average humans, the whole package weighs a good 350 pounds. Choose your trails carefully, and use your brakes frequently. The captain must remember that the stoker cannot see the trail ahead; abrupt and unexpected changes in terrain or speed can be, if not downright dangerous, at least uncomfortable and unsettling to the stoker. One-word warnings such as "Bump," "Braking," or "Left," should suffice. Exclamations such as "Oh no!" or "Look out!" are not recommended.

Although most tandems are sized so that the roles of captain and stoker are not easily interchangeable, these lessons are best learned by having the captain bring up the rear for an hour or two. This brief change of perspective will prove most enlightening for both captain and stoker.

Like a happy marriage, it takes equal parts of patience, perseverance, and a sense of adventure to smoothly navigate a tandem offroad. And like a happy marriage, it will provide satisfaction that cannot be done justice with mere words. Whether it's sharing the thrill of navigating a particularly tough section of trail, simply reveling in the victory of another steep climb conquered, or feeling the rush of speed that only a tandem can provide, the experience is unlike any other.

THE ULTIMATE FAMILY VACATION

For some, tandem riding on backroads may seem an extreme form of family vacation. But let's look at what extreme *really* means. Consider the Romp family. In April 1999, this family of five set out from Shoreham, Vermont, with the intention of traveling to Homer, Alaska, on a bicycle

built for four. Mom, Dad, and the two oldest kids pedaled a Santana Quad, while the youngest, age three, was pulled behind. That little cross-country jaunt pretty much sets the standard for an extreme backroads biking holiday. Here's how Billy Romp described how it felt to reach their destination on October 1, 1999:

> Well, we have made it to Homer, Alaska, the end of the road. Our final day of riding dawned rainy and cold, but we pedaled the final few miles under clearing skies. The weather reflected our feelings at the end of this incredible trip. We were elated to reach a goal that we set more than three years ago, and the sheer anticipation of this moment had us grinning and laughing. We all said over and over, I can't believe we're finally here!
>
> But we were sad, too. The trip had a life of its own, and we loved it. We were different people for six months: on our own, bold adventurers, relying on our muscles to get us from town to town, state to state. Our rig attracted attention and helped us make friends with the nicest people ever. We proclaimed, "ANYTHING IS POSSIBLE!!" and backed it up with action. We had come to feel at home rolling down the shoulder of the highway, talking and singing and not knowing where we would lay our heads down that night. Now we would return to automobile travel, regular clothes, and normal activities.
>
> The Homer Spit is a flat, narrow spit of land with a campground or two, a Coast Guard station and, at the very tip, the Land's End Resort. It was here that about forty people were gathered, waving and screaming, hooting and hollering. They stretched a yellow ribbon across the road, and we rode through it slowly, savoring the moment. We wheeled the bike down to the water and ceremoniously dipped the front tire into the waves. As we walked back up the beach, I looked for tears on Patti, Ellie, and Henry's cheeks. I'll never forget what I saw: the brightest twinkle in their eyes and the biggest smiles. Ellie half laughed, half said, "I can't believe—I mean I REALLY can't believe . . . we're finally here!"

I found it as hard to believe as Ellie Romp. So I wrote Billy and asked for the secrets of taking a *seriously* long family ride. Although he'd just completed the journey, he answered in full. Here's his advice on expeditionary cycling, family-style:

> Any bicycle tour that exceeds six or eight weeks in length may be termed an expedition. Equipment choices, financial arrangements, mental and physical preparation, choice of touring partners, and the like—factors that

determine the level of enjoyment on a shorter tour—will decide the success or failure of an expedition. Since we cyclists love to obsess about equipment, let's start there.

Reliability is key to every item, from the bicycle frame itself down to the smallest item of personal toiletry. This is no place for old or cheap equipment. On a six-month tour, you will be replacing parts, surely tires and drive-train components, but that doesn't mean you should carry a heavy inventory of parts with you. Unless you are traveling to the more remote reaches of the third world, you can easily arrange for shipment of replacement items. Find a bike shop at home that will take a telephone order and ship parts express to you, using your credit card for payment. Carry a phone number you can call for replacement of every critical piece of equipment, including camping gear, cameras, and the like. Using post office general delivery is the best method in the United States; in foreign countries, Federal Express to a hotel or embassy may be the best choice. Be sure you know the proper ordering information for every little part and gizmo: sizes, model numbers, and alternate choices that will work. Develop a small, highly refined emergency kit that will allow Yankee ingenuity to carry the day. I carry a couple of tubes, a folding tire, a patch kit, and a couple of cables, in addition to repair kits for clothing, panniers, tent, rain gear, and cookstove. My kit includes a fairly thorough tool set made up of individual quality tools instead of the multitools that, although lighter, aren't as versatile or durable.

Have a person who will act as mission control: someone who will get your mail and forward it, answer your phone, pay your bills, and act as a contact person. Forward your phone calls to mission control, and check in once a week or so. Try to arrange your life's details so that you will have as little to deal with as possible from the road.

On the road, you will be subject to the stresses of daily athletic activity, changes in diet, sleeping in a different place each night, exposure to weather, breathing automobile fumes, and other unforeseen factors. The accumulated stresses can cause fatigue, weaken your resistance to infection, affect your digestion and sleep, and produce other symptoms that may threaten your tour. By building basic health and fitness in the months (years?) before your tour, you will suffer less from these stresses. Attitude helps. Discard your expectations, go with the flow, and you will avoid stress, stay healthier, and enjoy more.

Perhaps no other decision will be as critical to the success of your expedition as the choice of a touring partner. But I can't help you there. Just remember: twenty-four hours a day, seven days a week, in challenging circumstances, your touring partner and you will be relying on each other for every little thing, and possibly some big things as well. You can put up with nearly anybody for a week or two. But for six months? Choose carefully.

For the full story of this extraordinary family and their amazing family trip, log on to www.rompfamily.com. And if you want to buy a caboose of your own, well, a good bike seat starts at around $100, a tow bar for a little less, and a covered trailer for $40 more.

FINDING THE PERFECT RIDE

Once you've decided to take a family outing, the next question is, where do you take it? How and where do you find the perfect ride? Here's Greg Danford's answer:

"You've got your bike and some essential gear, now you're ready to go. The only question is where. State forests, abandoned logging and mining roads, most public lands (with the notable exception of national parks), even private lands owned by accommodating landowners—all

With the wee bairn in Edinburgh.

make great places to ride. All you need to find the ride of a lifetime is a good eye, a little perseverance, and a well-developed sense of adventure.

"For starters, never stop looking. If you're driving and you pass a road that shows promise, make a note to return with your bike. (This practice often leads to arguments with my wife, who claims that I can't possibly be trail hunting and watching the road simultaneously.) I've even been known to search for trails from airplane windows, pressing my nose against the glass like a little kid.

"Second, keep at it. What may start as a difficult climb may level off into a wide-open meadow covered in wildflowers. You never know what kind of nirvana is around that next corner. Which leads to the adventure part. The more you go out and the farther you go, the more likely you are to find something spectacular. If you tried the left fork last time and it was great, try the right one this time—it may be even better. The point is that fun rides for all abilities are out there, and the riders who look the hardest are the ones who find them."

BIKE TRAILS

One of the great heroes of American biking is a lawyer who worked for the National Wildlife Federation. When he was a teenager, David Burwell watched as his mother, Barbara, and her friend, Joan Kanwisher, got the town of Woods Hole, Massachusetts, to buy a length of unused railroad line and turn it into a beachfront walking and cycling path. Inspired by the memory, in 1986 David left the NWF to found Rails-to-Trails Conservancy. The mission of Rails-to-Trails is to duplicate his mom's success in the rest of the country. By 1999, Rails-to-Trails had established some 10,000 miles of public recreation paths in forty-nine states. Pennsylvania alone has more than one hundred rails-to-trails running 867 miles within its borders, with nearly twice that mileage still to come.

The beauty of Rails-to-Trails for family cycling is that it's guaranteed never to get too steep—after all, it was made for trains. That lack of grade means that the weakest member of the family is unlikely to throw a tantrum in the middle of a ride because he can't make it up a hill! For more information, contact the Rails-to-Trails Conservancy at (202) 974-5100, or visit their website at www.railtrails.org.

Another important movement is the Greenway Alliance, which is establishing bike trails up and down the country. Today you can ride its rail trails in Maryland, New Jersey, Connecticut, and Rhode Island. By the year 2010, you should be able to cycle on hard-surface, off-highway trails from Calais, Maine, to Key West, Florida. If you want to help make this a reality, visit the website www.greenway.org.

Want even more of a challenge? The Adventure Cycling Association, a nonprofit organization dedicated to on and offroad cycling, has mapped a more than 2,400-mile ride from Canada to Mexico, right through the Rocky Mountains. Called the Great Route, it follows fire roads, jeep trails, single track, and occasional paved stretches, and it's guaranteed to stretch the limits of any mountain biker. For information or maps on the world's longest mountain bike route, visit www.adv-cycling.org.

Canada is making great strides toward a cycle-friendly society. In many ways, they're ahead of the States, which is one reason why they're so well represented in this book. Each province has its own rails-to-trails and other biking programs. For example, British Columbia features the Kettle Valley Rail-Trail, which covers 600 kilometers through the beautiful mountains of Canada's westernmost province. Besides the scenery, you ride through dark tunnels and traverse high trestles.

The Trans Canada Trail is on its way to becoming a shared-use recreation trail that will wind its way through every province and territory. It will be the longest trail of its kind in the world, spanning approximately 16,000 kilometers. The trail, which is already on its way to completion, will accommodate five core activities: walking, cycling, horseback riding, cross-country skiing, and snowmobiling. The Trans Canada Trail will be built on existing trails wherever possible, assuming they accommodate the shared-use principle; provincial and federal parks and crown lands on or alongside abandoned railway lines; and private land where rights-of-way can be negotiated with the landowners. For more information, visit the bilingual website at www.tctrail.ca.

For an update on cycling in Quebec, check out the Velo Quebec website: www.velo.qc.ca. A video in English or French is also available about their program.

BIKING PARADISE

If you're really committed to cycling, consider moving to Holland; Portland, Oregon; or Montreal. Holland has bike lanes everywhere, and nearly the entire country is on cycles. Portland has used city planning, persuasion, and 1 percent of its gas tax to set up 185 miles of bike paths into downtown and along prime waterfront land, bike racks on the city's buses and commuter trains, showers at health clubs, and cheap, safe bike parking all over town. As a result, Portlanders routinely bike to work and are three times as likely as other Americans to cycle to the store, to the Laundromat, to school.

As for Montreal, *Bicycling* magazine named it North America's number one city for cycling and cyclists. It's a city of well-marked bike lanes, municipal bike racks, a cycling citizenry, and knowledgeable bike shops. It's in a region of bike races, family outings, and a rich cycling culture. Montreal has more than 200 miles of bike paths and lanes. Montreal is also the hub of La Route Verte, an extensive network of bikeways that link with routes in New York and Vermont. And it's the home of the world's biggest gathering of cyclists, *Le Tour de l'Ile,* an annual event that each spring draws over 45,000 riders. For more info, check out www.velo.qc.ca and www.tourisme-montreal.org.

Other bike-friendly paradises include Denmark; Victoria and Vancouver, British Columbia; and Prince Edward Island. Note that a number are in Canada, whose climate is hardly what most would regard as ideal for serious cycling. Yet Canadian cyclists are undaunted by long winters. Let them be your example as you lengthen the days per year that you and your family take to your bikes.

BIKE CLUBS AND TOURS

Wherever you live, there's likely to be a cycling club not far away. Some clubs are set up for racing, some for road biking, some for backroad and offroad adventure. A fair number cater to all these pleasures. Others are willing and able to, once you join and say, "Backroads, anyone?" You can find your nearest bike club at www.Bikelane.com.

Bike tours can be enjoyable family events and can turn strangers into lifelong friends. I've been on a number of such tours, and I've met delightful people along the way. That's one of the tour's great appeals. Another is the sag wagon, the van that follows the group for those who need a lift for the next 10 miles or up to the top of the next hill. A third sweet aspect of the organized tour is that you get to stay in the wonderful little out-of-the-way inns, eat sumptuous home-cooked meals, and after supper, spend the evening chatting with new friends.

CHAPTER 8

Extending the Biking Season

Though biking is usually seen as a summer pastime, that season can be extended almost indefinitely. In other words, you can bike much longer than you think you can bike. Anyone can cycle comfortably when the temperature drops into the fifties, the forties, even the upper thirties. How? By dressing right. As the temperature drops, start progressively covering more body parts. Over your bike shorts, wear tights. Under your bike gloves, wear glove liners. Over your jersey, wear a fleece, and under it, wear a wicking undershirt. Under your helmet, wear a ski hat. If you wear bike socks, switch from CoolMax to wool.

As the temp drops further, add layers. Just as in other cool-weather sports, layering is the secret to cycling comfort. As the days grow colder, add jackets, sweatpants, neck gaiters. If the weather grows warmer, start peeling. One garment that makes peeling easy is Arm Skins, made by DeFeet. These cover your arms on frosty mornings, then roll down into wrist rolls when the sun comes out.

WINTER MOUNTAIN BIKING

Once you're hooked on cool-weather riding, the next step is snow riding. Larry Reed, a CPA and winter bike fanatic from Chester, Vermont, tells how—and why—he does it:

> With the right equipment and conditions, mountain biking during the winter months can be more exhilarating and challenging than biking the rest of the year. Because I enjoy road biking during the nonwinter months, and Vermont winters tend to be long, my mountain bike gets most of its use when there's snow on the ground. When I tell this to friends, they usually say I must be a little nuts.

103

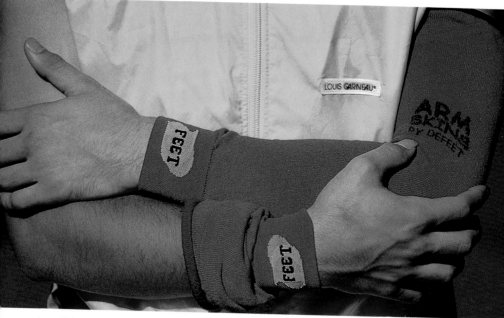

Arm Skins.

Maybe I am. But with studded tires, warm clothes, and the right weather conditions, I can go places closed to the public the rest of the year. That's because I ride on snowmobile trails that wander through forest and field, over frozen lakes, and beside snow-covered streams. The ideal weather for winter biking is warm days above 35 degrees and cold nights below 25 degrees. That combination allows the trails to harden overnight for ideal riding conditions during the early-morning hours. But riding on slippery surfaces requires excellent conditioning, above average agility and bike handling skills, and most of all, common sense.

The ideal conditions for riding fast on snow are generally found during the months of March and April, when the right combination of warm days and cold nights are most prevalent. It also helps to have some rain or sleet prior to a cold spell, which creates cementlike conditions on the trails. Beware of hoarfrost and other soft spots when riding after a warm spell. Also beware of ice under freshly fallen snow. I recommend not wearing cleats on your shoes so that you can dismount quickly and avoid

OPPOSITE: **Cool-weather gear.**

a head-over-heels experience if the front tire sinks into a soft spot. Be aware that as in any sport that involves downhill speeds on snow and ice, you are taking a certain amount of risk.

When riding on snowmobile trails, always yield to snowmobiles. You can hear them coming, but they can't hear you. Because the best conditions for mountain bike riding on the trails are early in the morning or late in the afternoon when the trails are set from the cold, you tend to avoid the snowmobiles. When I hear them coming, I remove myself and my bike completely off the trail until they pass by.

When the snowmobile trails are too soft to ride, dirt backroads can be just as much fun. Be sure to wash the road salt off your bike and components after each winter ride. I learned the hard way, having to replace front and rear derailleurs much sooner than expected.

Besides a helmet and protective eyewear, you'll need cold-weather booties to put over your shoes, and moisture-wicking clothing with zippered tops put on in layers—you'll sweat profusely on the climbs and need to zip-up on the descents. Use a hydration system rather than a water bottle for fluids. When worn under a layer of clothing, the fluid will not freeze; a water bottle will. It helps to have a front-end shock absorber. I have both front and rear suspension, which adds to the fun. You also should have studded tires.

Larry's friends may think he's crazy, but that's only because they haven't experienced the next step on the ladder of madness, winter boardercross racing. When a ski area hosts such a race, the riders take their bikes up on the lift, then race wheel-to-wheel down a course that includes great mounds of snow piled high enough to induce liftoff at the top. Winter bike racers spend nearly as much time in the air as on the snow.

The secret to handling a bike on snow is snow tires. Some come with heavy treads, others with metal studs. A good source is the WinterCycling webpage at aws@mosquitonet.com.

•FAQ• **When I'm downshifting or upshifting, can I skip gears, or do I have to run through the whole sequence, one at a time?** Skipping a gear here and there isn't the end of the world, but to prolong their lives and to avoid throwing a chain, don't race through the gears. If you can stop, even briefly, at each cog along the way, they'll thank you for it with a long and useful life. ■

OPPOSITE: Going up!

CHAPTER 9

Bike Care

The most costly mistake in backroad bike care is probably the most commonly made. After every mountain bike race or event, you'll see a long lineup of mud-splattered cyclists waiting for their turn at the high-pressure hose. When they reach the front, they turn the water on their bike, removing grit, sand, mud—and years of their bike's life. For while they're cleaning the outside, they're causing two kinds of problems on the inside.

If you must use a high-pressure hose, aim it only at the wheels and rims.
OPPOSITE: **Coming down.**

First, the water is seeping into the frame. Though some frames have a hole in the bottom to let water out, many—including expensive, high-end steel frames—do not. What the hosing does is introduce a rusting agent to your trusty cycle, causing it to rot from the inside out.

Second, as they put the jet of water to the wheel hubs, the hosers are not only removing dirt, they're blasting out the lubrication that keeps the hubs turning smoothly. Before long, they'll be replacing hubs, an expensive and time-consuming process.

A better method is to wait until the mud dries and brush it off with a gear-cleaning brush, a paintbrush, or a rag. Then reapply lube, and off you go!

If you still feel you must use that high-powered hose, point it only at the rims and tires. Mud comes off easiest when wet, and the spray won't damage these sturdy parts.

There are two attitudes toward bike maintenance and repair. Mine is this: For easy stuff that won't harm your bike if you mess up, learn to do it yourself. For preventive maintenance, learn to do it yourself. For truing wheels, changing cogs, or installing a new chain, go to an expert.

The alternative view is best described by Lennard Zinn in the introduction to his book *Zinn and the Art of Mountain Bike Maintenance.*

"Why do it yourself? There is an aspect of bicycle mechanics that can be extremely enjoyable in-and-of itself. . . . There is real satisfaction in dismantling a filthy part that is not functioning well, cleaning it up, lubricating it with fresh grease, and reassembling it so that it works like new again. Knowing that I made those parts work so smoothly, and that I can do it again when they get dirty or worn, is rewarding. I am eager to ride hard to see how they hold up, rather than being reluctant to ride for fear of breaking something."

In this chapter, I'll explain simple but essential repairs like fixing a flat, adjusting brakes, and fine-tuning gears, as well as preventive maintenance to keep you from having to make many major repairs. If, like Zinn, you want to do it all yourself, you should buy a repair manual. And I know of none better than *Zinn and the Art of Mountain Bike Maintenance.* It's so clear, in word and picture, that it almost made a convert of me.

It's preferable to do any necessary repairs at home rather than on some wilderness trail, and the way to avoid repairs out in the bush is to keep your bike maintained at home or, if you don't want to do it yourself, at your local bike shop.

OPPOSITE: **An easy way to get the bike down stairs.**

HOME REPAIR

Beyond the simplest maintenance, to do bike repair with any efficiency, and without the strong language that inevitably accompanies bleeding knuckles, requires specialized tools. Fortunately, they don't cost too much.

Start with a good, solid bike stand. Holding your bike where you can get to it without stooping or crawling will save your back. By making the part you're working on accessible, the stand will save your temper. Like a good woodworking vise, a repair stand makes the job cleaner and easier. Park Tool usa, the biggest manufacturer of bike-repair gear, sells the PCS-1 Home Mechanic Repair Stand for about $150. What's especially nice about it for the home repair shop is that the PCS-1 folds up for storage; most homes can't handle a big-based bike stand in the middle of the dining room.

Rather than assembling a tool kit on an as-needed basis, I suggest buying a ready-made kit. Park Tool's BK-2 Roll-Up Workshop costs about $125. It contains all the essential tools yet is portable enough to roll up and take to the driveway repair shop on a sunny day. While there are more elaborate and expensive kits on the market, including Park Tool's AK-32 Advanced Mechanic Tool Kit at $260, the work most of us are willing to tackle can be handled by the Roll-Up model. For those who don't want to spend money on a lot of tools, Park Tool's portable Micro Tool Boxes start at $8.

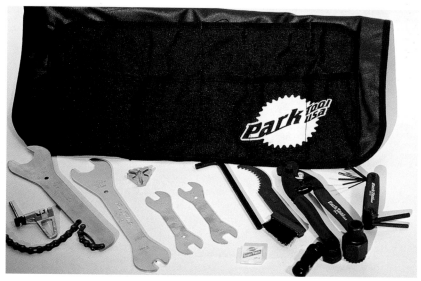

Roll-Up Workshop. Left to right: chain tool, chain whip, wrenches, spoke wrench, 8 milimeter hex wrench, patch kit, gear brush, crank wrench, cable cutter, lockring tool, bottom bracket tool, hex wrenches.

Opposite: Bike on repair stand.

The tools in the Roll-Up handle most jobs and include the following:
- cable and housing cutter
- chain whip and freehub lockring tool
- gear-cleaning brush
- chain tool
- crank wrench and puller
- Shimano cartridge tool and 8-millimeter hex wrench
- cone wrenches
- triple spoke wrench
- glueless tire patch kit
- tire levers
- open-end wrenches
- headset wrenches and pedal wrench
- hex set

Since these are the basic tools of bike repair, let's have a look at them and, more important, what to do with them.

Tools

Cable and Housing Cutter. Use this to snip brake and derailleur cables quickly and cleanly. You can get by with wire snips.

Cutting cable.

Setting up the chain whip.

Chain Whip and Freehub Lockring Tool. Most Shimano drive systems (gears and all that) hold the cogs (gears) in place with a freehub and lockring. To get to the gears, you have to first remove the lockring. To do so without bloodying your knuckles, hold it firmly in place with the chain whip while unthreading the lockring. That means wrapping the long section of chain over the top from the left side, using a middle-range sprocket. You don't need the chain whip when you reinstall.

Gear Brush. To get rid of grime and grit, stick the curved end in between the gears and pedal backward. Then use the brush to remove the loose dirt.

Chain Tool. It's next to impossible to repair or replace a chain without this tool. Its job is to push out and then replace a rivet, allowing you total access to the chain. First, to reduce tension, shift the chain onto the smallest freewheel cog and chain ring. Then set one of the chain's rollers into the chain tool, and turn the handle clockwise until the pin sits on a rivet. Keep turning until the rivet is nearly out; by leaving it in a just a bit, you can keep the chain together while repairing it. To reinstall the chain, reverse the procedure—unless your chain is a Shimano Hyperglide (HP) or Interglide (IP), in which case you *must* use Shimano's pin for reassembly. And you must use the right length pin. Or, if your chain is a Sachs P-C model, use their connecting link as described in their instructions.

Removing the lockring.

Brushing the cogs.

Brushing the teeth.

Popping a rivet.

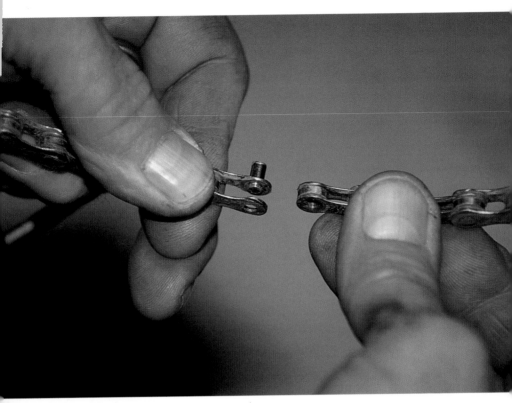

The rivet half-out.

Crank Wrench and Puller. To get at the bottom bracket, you've got to first take off the crank arms. Remove the dust cap, then remove the bolt beneath it with a 14-millimeter hex bolt or 8-millimeter socket head hex. Then screw the threaded end of the puller into the crank arm until it stops. With a wrench, turn the threaded post clockwise. With a few good turns, the crank arm will come off. When you reinstall, tighten securely to about 30 pounds of torque. (How tight is 30 pounds of torque again? Pretty damned tight. Bike technology is relatively simple technology. It tolerates imprecision pretty well. As a rule of thumb, the bigger the bolt, the tighter it should be.)

Shimano Cartridge Tool. To remove cartridge-style bottom brackets for replacement, screw the left-handed thread part of the tool into the drive side of the cartridge. *Remember, this is a left-handed thread!* When replacing, clean the threads, then Teflon-tape and grease the threads. And because this is a left-handed thread, be careful not to crossthread.

Removing the cranks.

Removing the bottom bracket.

Cone Wrenches. To work on axles without resorting to strong language, you need a cone wrench. Its most salient attribute is its thinness. While you adjust the outer locknut with a small or midsize wrench, hold the inner cone with the admirably thin cone wrench. Make your adjustments with the cone wrench, then tighten the locknut. Before you make that adjustment, though, lubricate the hub with bicycle grease.

Triple Spoke Wrench. The purpose of a spoke wrench is to true the bike's wheels, to make them perfectly round so they run true. The reason the wrench is triple is that spoke nipples (the parts you'll be adjusting) come in several thicknesses; these are the three most common. My strong advice is that unless you enjoy endless tinkering, leave the truing to a bike shop expert.

Tire Levers. The patch kit is the fastest, cleanest way of repairing punctures, which usually happen far from home. To get to that tube with a hole in it, first you've got to take off the tire. That's where tire levers come in. Slip the spoon end of the lever between the tire and the tube, being careful not to pinch the tube. By pushing the lever down, you pry the tire from the rim. Now, attach the hook end of the lever to a spoke. Move down the tire 6 inches and insert a second lever. Slip it in as well. Then slide the second lever along the rim, peeling off the tire. Be careful—the

Adjusting the axles with cone wrenches.

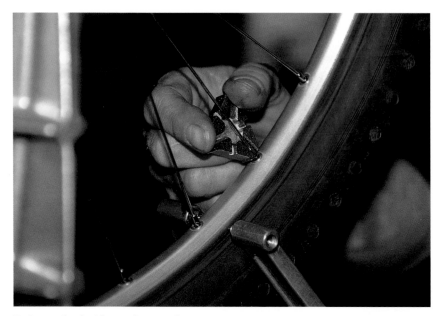

Truing a wheel with a spoke wrench.

Use tire levers, not fingers, to separate tire from rim.

bead edge of some tires is sharp enough to cut your fingers. That's why you use the levers. When you've peeled one side of the tire free from the rim, either work on the tube with the tire half off or peel the other side off by hand. If the tire is *really* on tight, use three levers.

Glueless Tire Patch Kit. Make sure the tube is clean and dry. Lightly sand the area around the puncture (sandpaper is included in the patch kit). Wipe off the sanded area until it's once again clean and dry. Pull the backing from the patch, being careful not to touch the sticky side. Press it firmly over the puncture for ten seconds.

Partially blow up the tube before slipping it back in the tire. Then put the tire back on the rim—taking care not to pinch the tube between tire and rim.

Now fully inflate the tire. Slip the wheel back into the forks, tighten the nut, and tighten the quick release. Reattach the brake cable. And away you go!

Hint: For rear-wheel punctures, work the chain to the smallest chain ring and cog before you start playing with the wheel; that takes the tension off the chain and makes wheel removal easier. Put back in forks, tighten the nut and tighten the quick release. Reattach the brake cable.

Headset Wrenches. These work like the cone wrenches, only now the purpose is to adjust the headset, the piece that keeps the handlebars attached to the rest of the bike. They're the same sort of wrenches, only bigger, for the same sort of cone and locknut. When you adjust the headset, find the sweet spot; it should be tight enough that there's no play (wobble) and loose enough that the

Hold the patch for ten seconds.

Don't pinch the tube between tire and rim.

This is why you carry a pump.

handlebars turn smoothly and easily. To test for play, roll the bike forward, then squeeze the front brakes. If there's play, you'll feel the knock of loose bearings. To test for smooth rotation, lift the front of the bike and rotate the handlebars. If you feel tight or sticky spots, loosen up.

If your headset is of the threadless variety, the adjustment parameters are the same but the tools are different. Use an Allen wrench to loosen the stem and to tighten the bolt in the top cap. Tighten it just a quarter of a turn at a time; if you tighten it too much, you'll break the top cap.

Pedal Wrench. Pedals can be devils to remove. A good pedal wrench helps by providing decent leverage and a tight fit. When you're using it, remember that the off-side pedal (the one without the chain ring) has *reverse threading*. With regular threading, when you turn a screw to the left, you loosen it; to the right, you tighten it. The off-side pedal is just the opposite. This knowledge should prevent you from inadvertently tightening the pedal until it's virtually welded to the crank.

Note that the chain is on the big chain ring.

Here are a few pedal tips: Grease the threads before reinstalling, and keep the pedals tight. To get them good and tight (and to get them off), use both pedal wrenches for added leverage. Before attempting to remove the right-side pedal, put the chain on the big chain ring. If the wrench slips, it could save you a trip to the emergency room.

Hex Set. This is your all-around bike tool kit. You need it to adjust the saddle, the handlebars, stems, brake, and derailleur bolts, and to install the bottle cage, mirror, and a host of other accessories. In the picture of the Roll-Up tool kit, the hex set is on the far right. Have one with you at all times.

Other Tools. You'll also need a tire pump with a gauge and the usual fixer-upper tools: screwdrivers, Vise Grips, needlenose pliers, hacksaw, hammer, and bench vise.

BACKROAD REPAIR

OK, that's what you keep in your shop, where the light is bright, the temperature is moderate, and where—this is the kicker—weight doesn't matter. But what about on a trip, off in the woods or on some lonely backroad? Even with scrupulous shop maintenance, flats happen, brakes break, cables snap. Wherever you least want them, problems arise. What should you take with you?

Basically, there are two schools of thought on the matter. Here's what serious repair expert Lennard Zinn carries on a short bike ride: spare tube, tire pump or CO_2 cartridge, two or three plastic tire levers, patch kit, chain tool, spare chain links, at least two subpin rivets for Shimano chains, small screwdriver, compact set of Allen wrenches, 2–6-millimeter, 8-millimeter and 10-millimeter open-end wrenches, spoke wrench, matches, identification, and cash for food and phone calls.

And here's what I carry on a short bike ride: water and an energy bar. Doesn't that get me in trouble? Just once, when I punctured a tire on a woods road. If I'd had a patch kit and tire levers, I wouldn't have had to push my bike the mile or two home, but I'd have carried them, oh, five hundred times for that one use.

On short rides—say a morning-long trip—I travel extremely light. As the trip grows longer, I add items, though I still travel light. If I'm alone, I attach a taillight flasher to the back of the frame. I take along a bit of money, a Swiss Army knife, and a portable wrench set. I toss in extra energy bars. And I increase my water supply from a bottle to a backpack hydration system. It's true that I won't be able to do any serious repairs, but there's a lot you can do without any tools at all, or with just a coin or a screwdriver.

Flossing the cogs.

Wiping the chain.

The first thing you can do is clean and lube the moving parts. Use a rag (or if you don't have a rag, then a stick, vine, or wad of leaves) to clean between the cogset, those toothed disks that transfer power from the chain to the wheels. Like human teeth, the disks need flossing, so just use an old rag as dental floss for cogs.

Cleaning the chain takes another rag. Turn the pedals backward with one hand while guiding the chain through a rag with the other.

If you hate touching all that oily, gunky chain stuff, buy a chain cleaner, a clear plastic reservoir for cleaning solution with holes at each end to run the chain through. But that's not for carrying into the woods.

After you've cleaned the chain, lubricate it by dripping oil or better, bike lube onto each link. Wipe off the excess.

Next, check to make sure everything's tight. You have either quick releases or bolts holding the wheels on and keeping the seat up. Check them for tightness, and if the quick-release skewer on the front wheel is pointing down, turn it until it points sideways or up. That will keep it from snagging a root on the trail, with instant consequences for the rider.

Now, adjust your brakes. You don't even have to get down on your knees to do it. How do you know if they need adjusting? Cycling at slow speed, say 10 miles per hour, squeeze one brake hard. If it can't bring the tire to an instant stop, it needs tightening. If the brake shoe rubs against the wheel rim when you're not squeezing the brake, it needs either loosening or repositioning. To adjust the brakes, simply turn the adjusting barrel,

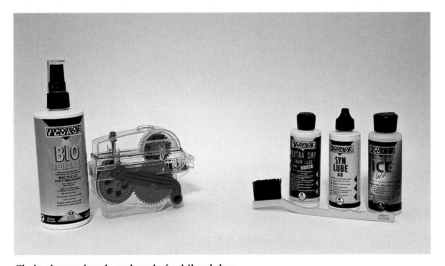

Chain cleaner, brush, and made-for-bikes lubes.

the round gizmo that attaches the brake lever to the brake cable. Then do the brake test again. Keep fiddling until it's right.

Now do the same for gears. This is a little trickier, but not much. Turn the bike upside down or hang it on a tree branch. Shift the chain to the big front chain ring and the rear derailleur to the smallest cog. Then shift to the second-smallest cog. If the chain is reluctant to make the shift, turn the barrel adjuster, which connects the shifter to the cable, counterclockwise. If the chain overshifts—skips the second cog entirely—turn the barrel adjuster clockwise. Keep playing with it until the chain moves smoothly between cogs. Now shift the chain to the middle front ring and go through the drill again. Do the same for the small front ring.

If the problem persists, you'll have to go to the derailleurs. But even here, all you need is a screwdriver. If you're doing this at home, use a bike stand. On both the front and rear derailleurs is a pair of screws called the limit screws. On most bikes, one is marked H, and the other L. These stand for high and low. Their function is to limit the sideways run of the chain so

Adjusting the brake barrel.
OPPOSITE: **Lubing the chain.**

Adjusting the shifter barrel.
Opposite: **Adjusting the rear limit screw.**

it doesn't jam into the bike frame or spokes in one direction and wedge itself between the smallest cog and the dropout in the other.

On the rear derailleur, loosen the H screw a quarter turn at a time until the chain shifts smoothly. If the chain whizzes past the smallest cog, tighten the H screw a quarter turn. Keep playing with it until all is well.

The L screw keeps the chain from racing past the cogs in the other direction and ending up tangled in the spokes. If that's happening to you, shift the chain to the inner front chain ring and the rear derailleur to the biggest cog. Tighten the L screw until it no longer overshoots. If it then has trouble climbing onto the biggest cog, loosen it again. Play with it until you find the ideal position.

The screws on the front derailleur also keep the chain from straying—in this case, from straying outside or inside the limits of the chain rings. If, when you shift, your chain falls off the rings to the inside, tighten the low-gear screw by turning it clockwise a quarter turn. If the chain won't shift onto the inner ring, loosen the same screw the same quarter turn. But if the chain makes a leap for freedom over the big chain ring, tighten the high-gear screw; if the chain is a slacker about climbing onto the big chain ring, loosen this screw.

Adjusting the front limit screw.

Finally, picture this. You're bombing along out in the woods when you take an endo, a head-over-heels fall. When you collect your body parts and your thoughts (which you'd no longer have if you weren't wearing a helmet), you discover to your horror that your beloved bike's front wheel is so thoroughly bent that you couldn't even think of riding it home.

What do you do now? One of two things. If there are some close-growing trees nearby, insert the wheel between two of them and bend it straight.

If not, take the wheel off the bike. Firmly grasping the rim, lift it high over your head. With considerable force, *whomp* it down on a flat piece of ground. Either way, you'll straighten it out enough for a slow and careful ride back home. The first thing you should do after taking care of your own wounds is to buy a new wheel.

•FAQ• **How do I know which lube to use?**

Andrew Herrick, former president of Pedro's USA, a leading bike lube company, answers:

"The key word is *conditions*. As a quick rule of thumb, use a dry lube when it's dry and a wet lube when it's wet. But to complicate things, Pedro's makes two different wet lubes: one for road biking and one for

mountain biking. The mountain bike lube, Synlube ATB is a medium-thickness lube that is great at coating the chain to protect it from the elements on a dirty trail. The road bike lube, Synlube ROAD, is a bit thinner so it penetrates better into the links of your chain for smoothness.

"We also make two different dry lubes: Extra Dry and Ice Wax. Extra Dry is not a wax; it's a biodegradable lube with Teflon. Extra Dry lube is for both road and mountain biking under superdry conditions.

"If it's a clean drivetrain you're after, wax lubricants like Ice Wax are by far the best. Wax lubes tend to be self-cleaning, as they fall off the chain over time, taking the dirt with them. This means more frequent applications, but cleanliness is central to drivetrain performance." ■

•FAQ•   OK, I've lubed my chain. Now what should I use to lube the rest of the bike—cables, pedals, and stem?
The two worst choices are chain wax and WD-40. Wax will clog the cables, and WD-40 is a solvent, not a lubricant. 3-in-One oil is a lubricant, but a cheap, all-purpose one without much lasting power. Your best choice is a purpose-made bike chain lube. ■

Opposite: **Whomping a wheel.**

CHAPTER 10

Rider Care

Here are some general bike safety tips that could save your brain and body:

- Always wear a helmet.
- Make sure your bike has front, rear, pedal, and spoke reflectors.
- Wear bright clothes at night, and use a light.
- Signal well before making a turn.
- Signal drivers when it's safe to pass. Make drivers your friends.
- Ride with traffic, not against it.
- Ride single file.
- Keep a sharp eye out for street hazards such as storm drains, trolley or train tracks, or parked car doors suddenly opening in front of you.
- Use caution on wet road surface, wet leaves, loose gravel, and newly honed dirt roads.
- Try to resist the temptation to weave in and out of stalled traffic. It's hard not to gloat, I know, but do your best to avoid further enraging already enraged drivers. They have a lot bigger vehicle than you do, as they may remind you when the traffic jam finally unsnarls. Willie Weir put it best in his book, *Spokesongs:* "I have learned the most important rule of the road: the bigger vehicle *always* has the right of way. This puts bicycles at the very bottom of the vehicle caste system."

You need to be extra careful when riding on wet roads. While mountain bike and hybrid tires are relatively wide, that's relative only to road and racing bike tires. The fact is, you're balancing a lot of weight on a pair of very narrow supports, and wet surfaces can easily lead to a spill. What's more, brakes don't work as well when wet, you can't see as far in the rain, and all in all, H_2O adds to the risk factor.

But that doesn't mean that rainy days aren't bike days. Cycling through gentle drizzle is one of the pleasures of cycling. You're cooled and refreshed even as you grind up an endless climb. The smell of rain in the air is alluring, and you're enjoying the outdoors while others are sinking into the springs of their couches. Just take a bit of extra caution, and you'll love cycling through soft rain.

SEX AND THE CYCLIST

In August 1997, the cycling world took a powerful hit—and not on the head. A big-circulation cycling magazine, *Bicycling*, came out with a story by leading cycling writer Joe Kita about the findings of Irwin Goldstein, M.D., a urologist with a special interest in impotence. Based on his studies and his patients, Goldstein concluded, "Men should never ride bicycles. Riding should be banned and outlawed."

This in a cycling magazine! What brought Dr. Goldstein to his chilling conclusion was that in an average week he saw six men who had become impotent from bike riding. He estimated that there were 100,000 more out there who had lost the ability to get or maintain an erection because "of penile damage inflicted by either the bike's top tube or its saddle." The article went further: While the evidence was still anecdotal, women, too, were complaining of sexual problems caused by cycling. Among them were labial chafing, numbness, and clitoral changes. Goldstein concluded, "If a woman likes the function of her clitoris, then perhaps bike riding is not in her best interest either."

As if that one-two punch weren't enough, the Kita article was accompanied by one written by one of the magazine's staffers, who candidly described how his years of racing and 21,000 annual miles in the saddle had rendered him "as soft as overcooked rigatoni." Now he was riding a recumbent bike and hoping he could return to full erections without surgery.

Since August 1997, a number of items have appeared on television, in the press, and online about cycling and sexual damage. Some dispute the Goldstein assertions on the grounds that his research methods were wanting; his conclusions were unwarranted; he failed to account for age, depression, and disease; other bike and health experts have not been inundated by riders suffering from sexual disorders; and even if you can't get it up, if you've been cycling, you've still got your health.

All this sounds fine until you see the pictures. If you look at the X-rays of impotent riders, it quickly becomes clear that the penile artery and nerves have been compressed either from an encounter with that round metal top tube or from pressure on the seat. That artery is the pipe through which flows the blood that engorges the penis and produces an erection. No open pipe, no blood. No blood, no erection. But why?

When you sit in a chair, your body weight is resting on your sit bones. But on a bicycle seat—and particularly on a narrow seat—the weight rests between the bones, on the perineum. That's where the blood-supplying vessels and nerves are, and they're crying out, "Don't tread on me!"

As of now, the data are far from conclusive. But my assumption is that Dr. Goldstein is on to something serious. So here are my suggestions to prevent impotence, labia chafing, and other disorders created between bike seat and bottom.

First, don't ride obsessively. Don't do anything obsessively—it's just asking for trouble. Mix cycling with skiing, swimming, walking, and maybe even reading a good book now and then.

Second, if you feel your genitals tingling or going numb, get out of the saddle. Either walk around a bit or get up on the pedals. Even if your special parts don't feel like pins and needles, get up on the pedals every ten minutes or so to give your bottom a break.

Third, change your seat. If the horn is up, lower it to level or a little below level. If you're on a skinny seat, trade for a wide one. If it's hard, cover it with a gel cushion or trade for a soft one. Try out a seat with an anatomical hole in it.

Fourth, add springs. Suspension systems built into the seat, the seat stem, and the frame cut down on the jounce.

Fifth, straddle the bike to make sure your top tube is at least 3 inches beneath your crotch. Since mine was not, I padded it with bubble wrap. Looked like hell, but when I considered the alternative, I didn't mind a bit.

Get up on the pedals when cycling over roots, stones, railroad tracks, and washboard dirt roads. Save your genitals *and* your fillings.

Here's a follow-up to the *Bicycling* magazine staffer's personal story. In 1998, he told me this: "I have regained full function and am again riding an average of 14,000 miles per year on a conventional road bike, not a recumbent. By the way, Viagra works for most men who suffer erectile dysfunction from circulation restriction of any sort, including pressure from a bike seat. Viagra wasn't on the market when the original articles appeared in *Bicycling*. Today the consequences are not nearly as dire for those cyclists unlucky enough to have a problem."

GETTING FIT

Despite all the improvements in cycles, it still takes effort to make those pedals turn. If you're thinking of going on a tour, you'd better exercise first. You should certainly put in some bike time before you embark. Start gently and work up—up in time, distance, speed, and climbing uphill.

The bubble-wrap solution.

Starting gently means using low gears. Larry Fennell, a racer-turned-tour-guide, puts it this way: "It surprises many people to learn that when I'm getting in shape for a racing season, I don't even use the big front ring for the first 1,000 miles." If Larry can start gently, so can you.

There are two ways to get fit for cycling. One is to train in the off-season; the other is to get fit in the saddle. Quebec ski racer Jean-Marc Blais faced this choice when planning a cross-country ride. "We knew we could train and be miserable for a week in the gym or just get on the bikes and be miserable for a week on the road. Since we couldn't see any advantage to preplanned misery, we didn't train at all. And after a week of torture, we had a great time."

If a week of torture isn't your idea of a warm-up for a great time, you might consider turning your bike into a trainer. Essentially, there are two ways of doing it. One is to buy rollers, revolving drums you ride your bike on; the other is to buy a trainer, a stand you mount onto the rear of your bike that lets you pedal indoors with the rear wheel spinning in the air. Trainers cost from $80 to $250; rollers go for $150 to $230. Which one should you get? Equipment expert John Schubert recommends the rollers. A trainer will build strength, he says, but roller riding will make you a far smoother bicyclist. Riders who are unsteady on the road are more so on rollers. They're a great tool to teach ultimate smoothness.

But you needn't buy extra equipment to get that full-body workout. You can get it on the road. Here's how. On hills, get into higher-than-usual gear and stand up. Suck in your stomach. Pull on the handlebars with every downstroke. Use your arms as much as your legs to power you up the hill. But be careful—this is a powerful full-body workout, and you should build up to it gradually. Start with short bursts and less than full arm power. Otherwise, you risk the dreaded tennis elbow. Trust me, I know.

SPORTS NUTRITION

While writing a story on sculling at Vermont's Craftsbury Outdoor Center, I met Sunny Blende, an expert rower and mountain biker who is a practicing sports nutritionist with a master's degree in human nutrition. When she announced she was giving a talk that night on sports nutrition, I made it a point to come along. Was I glad I did! It turned out to be the only nutrition talk I'd ever heard that was both comprehensible and useful. On the spot, I asked her to write about the subject for this book.

The following information on nutrition is from her.

Whether you're biking a couple of miles on an easy trail or going up a mountain for three hours, your nutrition and training diet can be a major factor in your performance and enjoyment of the ride. Serious athletes who are training daily have special nutritional needs (getting enough calories for energy), but even recreation-level athletes have unique nutritional challenges. What and when you eat can turn a good mountain bike ride into a great mountain bike ride.

First the Basics

There are six essential nutrients for maintaining optimal health. They are carbohydrates, proteins, fats, vitamins, minerals, and water. The first three provide calories for energy and metabolism. Vitamins and minerals, although not a source of calories, work as catalysts that help regulate the body processes and reactions. They can also combine to form body structures such as calcium in bones. Water helps stabilize body temperature and is necessary for cellular functions, particularly carrying nutrients to cells and carrying wastes away.

Everything the human body does—including mountain biking—requires energy from the combustion of food and oxygen. This process called oxidation, or the burning of food, provides the fuel for our cells to work while also producing heat. How much fuel you need depends on your weight (lean body mass only; fat doesn't need fuel), your level of fitness (the more fit you are, the more fuel-burning components you have in your cells and therefore the higher your resting metabolic rate is), and the amount and intensity of the exercise you do. Obviously these factors can be changed, and the benefits of exercise like mountain biking become apparent.

Good Nutrition Training Diets

The important considerations for exercising individuals include adequate calories and carbohydrates. Athletes need to maximize carbohydrate stores, known as glycogen, for high-level activities such as races and strenuous exercise, as well as ongoing training, and they need to consume enough food to prevent their bodies from breaking down their own protein (such as muscles and tissues) for energy. For an active man or woman, a good goal is 60 percent of the diet from carbohydrates in nutritious foods such as breads, grains, fruits, and vegetables, thus supplying muscles with needed glycogen. Protein from low-fat sources such as fish, chicken, and dried beans will provide nutrients for building and repairing tissues and organs and should be 15 to 20 percent of the diet. The remaining 20 to 25 percent of the diet will come from fats, which should be mostly of the unsaturated types, and provides the body with a source of stored energy that can be used in all low-level activities, such as easy exercise, walking, or sitting.

Preride Meal

The food you eat before a workout functions to prevent hypoglycemia, or low blood sugar, with accompanying symptoms of lightheadedness; helps settle your stomach; and fuels your muscles with stored glycogen. Allowing enough time for food to digest before beginning to ride is important, because as blood leaves the stomach to go to exercising muscles, digestion slows down. The following guidelines should help:

- Large meal: 3 to 4 hours
- Small meal: 2 to 3 hours
- Liquid meal: 1 to 2 hours
- Snack: 1 hour

Eat familiar foods, about 1 to 4 grams of carbohydrate for every kilo-gram of body weight. For a 150-pound person, this could be a bagel with 2 tablespoons of jelly and 8 ounces of a sports drink. Eating a high-carbohy-drate diet daily will ensure that you're ready to ride anytime and make this ritual less important. Don't forget to hydrate! Drink lots of plain water.

During the Long Ride

Whether riding for fun or training for competition, mountain bikers can ride over distances and lengths of time that challenge their fluid and fuel levels. Fortunately, a cyclist can be more self-sufficient than other athletes can, in that food and drinks can be carried easily on the bike or in pockets and bike bags. A cage to carry a water bottle should be a necessity, not an accessory. Clearly, feeling good during a ride will mean looking after fluid and carbohydrate intake. In hot weather and with strenuous exer-tion, sweat losses can be high and can contribute to dehydration. It is important that you hydrate. How quickly the drink is absorbed can be more critical than how much you drink. Cold drinks leave the stomach quickly and are absorbed faster. Large volumes are absorbed quicker but may not be tolerated as well. Glucose and electrolytes, as in sports drinks, help absorption. They may also keep an athlete thirsty and drink-ing longer.

Rides lasting less than an hour can be managed with water alone as long as there's a recovery meal. But for longer or really strenuous rides or in warm weather, carbohydrates are needed to prevent the dreaded "bonk" or "hunger flat" that signifies fuel depletion. This is easiest in the form of sports drinks or a sports bar, along with water, but any food that provides fast energy will work. Bananas can really ripen in a pack, though, so plan ahead. The important recommendation to follow is to eat 1 gram of carbohydrate for every minute of exercise. Read the labels.

Recovery Nutrition

For ongoing training, daily recovery requires a diet high in carbohy-drates, but also clever timing of meals and snacks to restore the muscles with fuel for the next ride. The ability of muscle tissue to replace glycogen is greatest in the first hour following exercise. Eating within thirty min-utes is even better to keep the glycemic index high, because the muscles can store twice the amount of carbohydrates in this critical time. Simple and complex carbohydrates are equally effective in repletion, but com-plex carbohydrates have added benefits of fiber, vitamins, minerals, and decreased fat.

The target amount of recovery nutrition is $1/2$ gram of carbohydrate per pound of body weight within the first two hours after exercise, followed by the same amount two hours later. For a 150-pound person, 75 grams are necessary. Since 1 gram of carbohydrate equals 4 calories, this would be approximately 300 calories.

Alcohol has a dehydrating effect on the body and is a rather poor source of carbohydrates, despite popular belief. A 12-ounce, 150-calorie beer has only 50 carbohydrate calories. If you want to celebrate after a ride, hydrate first, have some food, and then have a beer.

Some Basic Guidelines

To help you prioritize what's important in your sports nutrition diet—and just for plain good health—follow these guidelines:

- Eat a balanced diet.
- Eat a wide variety of foods. This provides valuable small trace minerals, phytochemicals, and other nutrients you may miss if you eat the same things daily.
- Eat food as close to the source as possible—in other words, less processed foods.
- Eat more like a vegetarian, choosing lots of fresh fruits and vegetables. Usually, the more colorful the food, the more nutrients it has.
- If you are not that careful in your diet choices, take a supplement that has no more than 100 percent of the RDA, with the following exceptions or additions:
  Beta-carotene—25,000 IU
  Vitamin C—500 to 1000 mg
  Vitamin E—400 IU
- Drink lots of water—more than eight glasses a day.
- Moderation.
- Bon Appetit!

ALTERNATIVES TO EXERCISE

Sure, you're supposed to exercise before cycling. Some people do, you know. But for the rest of us, exercising to prepare for cycling is just another New Year's resolution: great in theory, admirable in intent, sensible as spinach, and impossible to maintain for more than two consecutive days.

The trouble is, for most of us, exercise is dead boring. The country is full of people who could cure their bad backs if only they'd stretch for twenty minutes each morning but who have discovered that exercise ennui is a worse fate than sacral suffering.

Why is exercise so excruciatingly dull? Because exercise is physical activity to promote fitness. And there's nothing as boring as doing one thing for the sake of something else, especially something else as worthy as fitness promotion.

And yet it seems to be true—performance improves and accidents lessen when the body is reasonably fit. Is there a way out of this dilemma? Yes. We simply have to find a means to get fit without exercise. The trick is to make physical activity do something more interesting or exciting.

The following are some ways to get ready for cycling without actually stooping to exercise.

Cross-country Skiing. Let us acknowledge that for adrenaline junkies, cross-country skiing is the equivalent of nonalcoholic champagne. That said, it's an activity that has many virtues. It uses most of the muscles of the body. It keeps you warm. It's free, or very nearly so. It's clean, white, fluffy, quietly exhilarating, and it keeps you moving during the time of year when most folks are hibernating in front of the TV.

Walking. Walking is actually rather good for you, and at the same time, it gets you places. Do not confuse walking with jogging, however, which may also be good for you but qualifies as exercise. Walking is particularly good preparation for cycling if you work a few extra things into it. Take long strides. Climb hills. Climb stairs, preferably two or three at a time. Make it a habit rather than a rare event. Remember, it's not exercise—it gets you where you want to go.

Dancing. Though it's every bit as physical, dancing is the complete opposite of exercise. In the history of the world, no one was ever bored when dancing with a sexy partner. Dancing is vigorous, exciting, romantic, sexually arousing, and still legal in most states. The difference between dancing and wrestling is that some holds are barred in wrestling.

Wrestling. Do this only if you can't dance.

Cycling. Oh, do not neglect cycling as a way of getting in shape for cycling. You use exactly the same muscles and have precisely the same amount of fun. And it's a proven fact, the more you bike, the more prepared you'll be for biking.

To add to the benefits of this activity, you might consider some warm-ups before hopping on the saddle, followed by a few decent stretches. Nothing painful or boring, of course. Not exercise. Just a bit of stomping around, swinging your arms in circles. Stretch your back in all directions and hold each position for half a minute or so. Stretch your calves on the curb for another minute. Then your thighs by grabbing your ankle and hauling it up behind your butt. That'll do it. Enjoy the ride.

Here's another alternative to exercise from Paul Kennett, one of New Zealand's leading mountain bikers:

"When I was going to high school in the late 1970s, I lived in Invercargill. That's the last city at the bottom of the South Island, at the bottom of New Zealand, which is not too far away from the bottom of the world. It's cold. Cold enough to make you want to stay in bed every morning. So I did.

"I timed the departure from my warm bed to the minute. I had ten minutes to get up, wash, get dressed, eat breakfast, and make my lunch. Then I'd jump on my one-speed and sprint 5 kilometers (that's 2 miles and a bit) to school, arriving at exactly 9 A.M. If there was a bitter antarctic headwind that morning, I'd just sprint harder.

"Of course, if it was a sunny midsummer morning, I'd be thinking, 'This looks like an easy ride today—so I can stay in bed a little longer.'

"After all those years of sprinting to school, I bought my first mountain bike in 1984, and I was suddenly quite a good rider—even managed to get to the New Zealand national champs in 1987.

"The moral of the story is 'sleep late, ride fast.'"

PREVENTING CYCLING INJURIES

Here's some advice on preventing cycling injuries from Steve Occleshaw, a Vancouver physiotherapist (what they call a physical therapist in the United States) and a dedicated cyclist.

As a physiotherapist, I commonly see recreational and elite cyclists with overuse injuries. These are long-standing or recurrent musculoskeletal problems resulting from repetitive overloading of body tissues. Several factors contribute to this type of injury: abrupt changes in exercise time or intensity, insufficient warm-up or cooldown, and lack of strength or flexibility.

These aren't the only factors, but they are ones that can be controlled. The most common sites for cycling overuse injury are the neck, knees, groin, buttocks, hands, shoulders, and lower back.

You can do a lot to prevent cycling injuries. Early in the season, remember that the body needs gradual increases in activity levels. Going from prolonged minimal activity to hammering the trails on the first day of summer is only asking for trouble. Here are some training tips:

- Build up time and distance slowly on the bicycle.
- Avoid excessive hill climbing early in the season.
- Pedal faster in easy gears rather than pushing heavy ones; riding at around 80 revolutions per minute maximizes energy output.

- Try to maintain general strength throughout the year.
- If you haven't been on your bike for a while, follow the "rule of tens." Start at about one-tenth the distance you were doing at the end of last year, and increase by 10 percent every other day.

Prior to exercise, it's important to perform a light warm-up and stretching routine. The warm-up can be as simple as a few minutes of marching on the spot (as goofy as it looks) or five minutes of easy pedaling. Incorporate some gentle shoulder/arm circles into the warm-up.

Once your muscles are warm, start your stretching routine. The goal of stretching is to relieve muscular tension and increase flexibility prior to exercise. If you are inflexible for your age, you should be more diligent with stretching, as shortened tissues are more likely to break down with activity. Use these rules for stretching:

- Keep the body part as relaxed as possible.
- Apply the force slowly and gently to the first onset of resistance.
- Maintain for at least twenty to thirty seconds.

You should generally stretch all the major muscle groups in the upper and lower body, as most of these areas are involved in cycling. The muscles that provide the power for cycling need extra attention. These include the gluteal (buttock) muscles, the quadriceps on the front of the thigh, and the long hamstring muscles down the back of the thigh. The calf muscles should still be stretched, even though they're not major power producers.

Also remember to cool down by spinning easily for five minutes at the end of your ride; then repeat your stretching. This gives your tissues a chance to properly flush out toxic by-products, thus limiting the delayed muscle soreness you feel later.

Following these simple ideas will reduce your chance of sustaining an injury. If you do have a recurring problem and the basic "RICE" principles—rest, ice, compression, and elevation—haven't dealt with it, consult your family doctor or physiotherapist. The longer the tissue damage goes on, the more difficult it will be to treat.

TREATING INJURIES

If you do sustain an injury from cycling, what's it likely to be, and more important, how should you treat it? For answers, I turned to Vermont physical therapist expert cyclist Phil Sweet. But before you read it, a cautionary note: The rather long list that follows consists of real potential injuries. But you should not come away from it feeling that this sport is too dangerous for you. For most people, cycling has cured far more problems

than it's caused. Most of us who ride to work, to relax, to get fit, to see the world put on endless miles without injury, without pain, without anything but pleasure. We save money, save fossil fuels, save at least a portion of the environment, and save our minds and bodies by biking. So read what follows as a lesson in preventive medicine, not as a grim message about the future of your body.

Here's Phil Sweet on biking injuries:

Apart from head injuries, which are best prevented by wearing a helmet and observing the rules of the road, there are a number of conditions associated with cycling. Here are the most common, and what to do about them.

Iliotibial Band Syndrome

On the outside of the thigh just above the knee is a tendon called the iliotibial band. It lies directly over the outermost portion of the femur, or thigh bone. The repetitive action of pedaling can cause the iliotibial band to rub across a portion of the femur called the lateral condyle, creating friction and stress. Inflammation and soreness may result. Remedies may include the basic RICE principles (see page 147). Stretching this tendon and its muscle near the hip often gives further relief. To decrease stress across the region, turn the toes out more while you're pedaling. Special clipless pedals may be needed in order to allow the toe-out position, and pedal extenders are sometimes needed in order to get the toes to turn out without the heel hitting the crank. A good bike shop can help set you up.

Neck Pain

Neck and upper-back pain are extremely common among cyclists of all abilities. The new cyclist may have additional reasons for complaining of neck pain. Early in the season, or as the novice's body is getting used to the bicycling posture, the muscles of the back of the neck are forced to support the head in an extremely forward-bent position. This creates excessive fatigue and stress in these muscles, leading to muscle pain and trigger point development. Trigger points are those sore, painful muscles that seem to radiate pain; those points of pain are usually due to overexerting an unused muscle. The weight of the helmet and biking's demands on the muscles of the shoulders and arm are enough to start injury in these muscles. The best way to prevent this type of injury is to avoid extremely long rides until these muscles have had a chance to become conditioned to the new activity. Strengthening exercises may be needed for the involved muscles. Lying facedown and raising the arms out to the sides as you lift them off the floor is a good initial upper-back strengthening exercise. Free weights will also generally condition the body for the bike season. Mechanical solutions may include altering the reach by changing the handlebars, shortening the stem, or moving the seat forward.

Lower-Back Pain

Lower-back pain, like neck pain, can be very serious; the lumbar disks are at risk for injury and herniation. Disk herniations are most common in the lumbar spine and are most frequently caused by excessive forward-bent posturing of the lower back—the position required in cycling. Decrease the bend by changing your seat position or handlebar height. Conditioning the muscles of the lower back by lying on the floor and slightly raising the arms and legs for counts of ten is a good way to strengthen these muscles.

Ulnar Neuropathy

In ulnar neuropathy, the ring and little finger experience numbness and tingling that persists even off the bike. Grip weakness is another symptom. You can correct it two ways. Wearing padded gloves is generally enough to improve minor problems with numbness and tingling. It also helps to change hand positions frequently, avoid extreme elbow positioning (either sharply bent or excessively straight), and shun extremely long rides in the early part of the season.

Carpal Tunnel Syndrome

Mechanical trauma to the median nerve, which runs along the palm side of the wrist, is not as common as ulnar compression. But the signs of carpal tunnel syndrome are similar: numbness and tingling in the long and index fingers and the thumb all along the palm side of the hand. Management is the same as for ulnar neuropathy, with special emphasis on adequately padded gloves.

Trochanteric Bursitis

This bursa lies over the hip bone and under a muscle called the tensor fascia lata. Injury is a result of the excessive rubbing of the muscle over the hip bone, or trochanter. Most frequently this is because the seat is too high; lower it until it decreases the stress to the bursa yet does not force the hips to rock excessively from side to side.

Biker's Knee, or Patellofemoral Pain Syndrome

This is an inflammation of the undersurface of the kneecap, or patella, and may be a result of poor alignment of the extensor mechanism (quadriceps, patella, and its tendon). Problems that the cyclist may inherently have are inflexibility of the hamstrings and/or quadriceps, high or lateral riding patella, or several varying types of postural misalignment that are most often congenital. Check the seat position; often it is too low or too far forward. And be sure you're not trying to push too hard a gear for the terrain you're on—keep that pedal cadence up above 80 revolutions per minute.

Patellar Tendinitis

This is inflammation and pain in the tendon that connects the kneecap, or patella, to the shin, or tibia. It is most common on the outside of the knee but can also occur on the inside portion of the tendon. Sometimes it is confused with iliotibial band syndrome because the areas of inflammation can overlap. Often the cyclist is riding too low or too far forward in the saddle, or the pedals may be turned in or out too much. Treatment is best done through minor, incremental adjustments to seat and pedal position. Be careful about off-the-bike activities, such as too much weight training.

Foot Parasthesias, or Numbness

This problem may simply be due to the wrong footwear. Shoes that cramp the feet or compress the forefeet or toes can cause the toes to become numb or tingle. It can often be alleviated by removing the feet from the pedals and turning the feet in circles while riding. Make sure your shoes aren't causing the problem. Before you run out and buy new shoes, try a thinner pair of socks.

Saddle Problems

Saddle problems may include severe skin irritations, including chronic folliculitis resulting from chafing, development of significant calluses; penile insensitivity possibly leading to male impotence; or inflammation of the urethra in males or urinary tract infections in females. Correction depends on the nature of the problem; it is best managed through close attention to the onset of any minor skin changes, numbness or tingling in the genitals, or changes in urinary activity or function. Choose a saddle that not only is initially comfortable but is soft or cut out in the front portion. Adequately padded riding shorts are also recommended.

Achilles Tendinitis

Although more common in runners, the Achilles tendon can become inflamed from habitually pedaling in a toes-pointed position. Onset can also be related to changing footwear or the pedal system. Leg length problems can lead to plantar fascitis on the short leg side and Achilles tendinitis in the long leg side. An expert in addressing such injuries in cyclists will be able to correct the leg length difference with inserts in one or both shoes.

Plantar Fascitis

This is a sore, painful foot arch that's usually worse in the morning when the feet first hit the ground. The pain often goes away after a few minutes of walking but will return if you are off your feet even for a few minutes. One common cause of this problem is a tight calf muscle, which can be effectively stretched while riding by standing on the pedals and letting your heel sag toward the ground until you feel a stretch in the back of the lower leg. Off-bike, try stretching the ankle by facing a wall and leaning into it until you feel your calf stretch. Physical therapists recommend having a foot and ankle evaluation to determine if you have any postural problems that set you up for such a condition.

•FAQ• Plantar fascitis sounds painful. How can I prevent it?

It *is* painful, as you're reminded every time your foot touches the ground. I developed plantar fascitis by taking long, strenuous rides while cycling without toeclips or clipless pedals. Climbing steep Vermont hills with the pedal under my arch had me hobbling.

My preventive measures are riding with the ball of my foot on the pedal and aggressively stretching my calf muscles.

Kate Carter suggested another solution. When I described my painful arch, she said, "Get yourself a pair of Dansko clogs! They'll prevent *and* cure plantar fascitis." They didn't, but they've become my after-biking shoe of choice. For plantar fascitis, keep your arch off the pedal, and keep stretching. ▪

CHAPTER 11

Competitions, Races, and Schools

For most folks, simply riding a bike is enough. Riding gives them exercise, adventure, transportation, and a chance to get away from the computer screen. As riding skills improve, your sense of balance gets better, your stamina extends, and your confidence grows. But others want more. They want challenge, in the form of a competition, race, an event, or school.

COMPETITIONS AND RACES

For cyclists at all levels above absolute beginner, racing and competing are fine ways to improve mountain biking skills. Furthermore, it's a chance to pick up tips by watching and listening to bikers who are far better riders than you. Mountain bike races are divided into categories. Here are the most popular:

Cross-Country. Uphill and down, often through muddy and rocky sections, the cross-country race is either a loop or point-to-point. It usually begins with a mass start and goes for 10 to 30 miles.

Endurance Events. For either a set time (usually eight, twelve or twenty-four hours) or a set distance (50 miles or more), racers ride against the clock and each other. Sometimes, instead of individuals, it's a relay team event.

Downhill. This is just like it sounds: The racers start at the top, and the first one down—by the stopwatch—wins.

Hill Climbs. This race is from the bottom to the top of the hill. Do a lot of strength and aerobic training before you try this one.

Dual Slalom. This is the same thing as a ski slalom race on TV on bikes. It's a side-by-side duel against the clock and the racer in the next lane.

Dirt Criterium. Nasty, brutish, and fun. After a mass start on a short course, riders try to lap the competition, and they circle the $1/2$-mile circuit time after time.

The dual slalom.

Time Trials. Competitors race one at a time against the clock. The course can be cross-country, downhill, uphill, whatever the race planners decide.

Observed Trials. If you want to build your bike-handling skills, look no further. In observed trials, the focus is not on speed but on tests like hopping a bike from tree stump to tree stump, climbing and descending a flight of stairs, and riding over a woodpile. The trick is to do it with the fewest touchdowns with hand or foot, called dabs.

Stage Race. The decathlon of mountain bike racing. Racers compete in a series of events, and the best cumulative score takes home the prize.

Freeriding. The extreme end of mountain biking. Involves cliffs, crevasses, couloirs, and other places sane people avoid. Great fun to watch.

Orienteering. Here's an event where map-reading skills are as important as bike-handling skills. Miss a check point and lose a race point. Miss enough and lose the race.

When the race is part of an event, such as a mountain bike festival, there are bound to be skill-building contests for kids, as well.

Here's what a typical race day is like. This one took place at Craftsbury Outdoor Center in northern Vermont. Ninety-one racers from New England, New York, and Quebec spent the last few minutes before the

Mountain-bike limbo builds skills.

An alternative use for a woodpile.

morning race breathing deeply, trying to swallow just a little more water, and pretending not to be completely wired.

At 10 A.M., the starter's pistol fired, and the expert group squealed off the asphalt tennis court and onto the adjoining soccer field. Two minutes later, they were scrambling up the short, rough slate hill behind the dormitories.

As the cyclists hurtled over the top, they picked up speed on the smooth, mown grass of a flat meadow. In one more minute, they hit the woods. By the time the last of the bunch disappeared into the pines, the sport group was awaiting the starter's gun. The beginners took off next, then the timed riders. By 10:15, everyone was racing.

Because the weather was dry, mud holes were few and relatively benign, but that didn't make the course a pushover by any means. Most of its 5 kilometers followed cross-country ski trails. In Vermont, that means long, fast downhills with sharp turns at the bottom, climbs tough enough to make the choice of whether to pedal or push a difficult decision, and enough surface variation in the form of loose stone, slippery grass,

There are events for big kids too.

cushiony mulch, and half-hidden logs to keep riders sharp-eyed. Flat tires started occurring in the first mile, and more than one rider who saved weight by not packing a spare ended up carrying a mountain bike back to the starting line.

Experts rode 20 kilometers. Male sport riders rode 15. Female sports, beginners, and timed-trialers rode 10. They all looked like they'd done a hard day's work by the time they crossed the finish line.

The best-known racer of the day came in ninth. Dr. Robert Arnot, the CBS television doctor, flew his single-engine plane up from New York to participate in the event. Ninth wasn't bad, considering that he had just returned from Bangladesh, where he'd interviewed everyone from the president to disaster victims, and he had just recovered from three broken ribs, an injury he'd received in another Vermont mountain bike race six weeks earlier.

After the last racer pedaled across the finish line, Craftsbury put on one of its famous chili lunches, followed by a drawing for prizes supplied by cycling and skiing companies. Then, at 1:30, the real fun began. It was time for the observed trials.

A corner of the meadow had been turned into a man-made obstacle course filled with logpiles, stairs, ramps, and platforms. Once the cyclists finished riding, climbing, descending, and balancing on these settings, they were invited back into the woods. That's when things got tough.

Whatever deviltry the course organizers could build into the man-made obstacles, Vermont's natural countryside could do worse. Much worse. A wooden stairway in a meadow doesn't compare with a natural stone stairway in the woods, especially when the stone stairs come complete with sharp edges, balancing rocks and sliding gravel. The ramp that had looked so tough was a pushover when compared with a nearly vertical cliff face in the forest. And the platform seemed positively puny once you saw the giant boulder the expert group was required to climb, balance precariously on, then leap off with both wheels at the same time, completing a half turn in the air so as to miss the big blue spruce 10 feet below it.

The observed trials gave trial cyclists a chance to hit the air and hit the ground. It gave them an occasion to watch their bikes crash through the trees in one direction while they plowed through the underbrush in another. It gave them an opportunity to practice humility—as well as humiliation. Strangely, most of them looked like they were loving every golden minute of it.

If this sounds like fun to you, consider going the next step and organizing a race of your own. Here's how Paul Kennett did just that in New Zealand:

> In 1984, the New Zealand national cycle touring magazine carried an article about "clunker bikes," and I bought one of the first fifteen mountain bikes imported into New Zealand. A lot of people thought I was crazy to pay $650 for "an oversized BMX with too many gears." But I'd read a few cycling magazines, and it was pretty clear to me that this was the next big thing.
>
> A year later, the handful of other offroad bikers I knew started saying that someone should organize a race. So I did. In an effort to attract every mountain biker in the country, I placed a full-page ad in the national cycling magazine and called it the 1986 National Off-Road Bicycle Championships. The course was the best hard-core adventure ride in the region. It included a 1-kilometer bike-*carry* section, aptly called the Devil's Staircase.
>
> My brothers and I have been organizing the Karapoti Classic on the first Sunday of March every year since. For the last few years, we've had to limit entries to one thousand riders, which we reckon makes it the biggest annual mountain bike event in the Southern Hemisphere. You can get more info at www.mountainbike.co.nz.

If you want more information about offroad racing, contact the National Off-Road Bicycle Association (NORBA). Your local bike store has details, or write USA Cycling, One Olympic Plaza, Colorado Springs, CO 80909, or visit their website, www.usacycling.org.

Jesse Terhune, a nineteen-year-old up-and-coming mountain bike racer, has this advice for potential racers:

"Don't overtrain. I did that last year and got nowhere; all I did was knock myself out. The best way to train is to ride two days in a row, skip a day, then ride two more days. Or, ride one, skip one, ride one, skip one. And ride by *time*, not by *miles*. Give yourself two or three hours, as opposed to 20 miles, of workout. That way you don't become obsessed with miles, like I did last year. I rode 4,000 miles and never improved. This year I've done better with less miles and shorter rides.

"I like to ride part roads, part trail. Roads build endurance; trails build skills. You definitely need the technical skills that roads don't give you, and you also need the heart and lung capacity as well as muscle development that you get from road riding.

"On the road, find your best rhythm. On the trail, develop your versatility."

MOUNTAIN BIKE SCHOOLS

A list of mountain bike schools can be found on the Internet. I've been to one in southern Vermont called Mount Snow, which offers weekend or four-day sessions.

A school for mountain bikers is a high-risk idea. There are two problems: Everybody already knows how to ride a bike. And mountain bikers—even those who started yesterday—hate to admit that they weren't born in the saddle. To confess that they don't already know how to jump a log, ford a stream, or scramble up a slippery slope is just short of coming right out and saying, "I am a nerd who'd be better off on a tricycle."

Fortunately for Mount Snow, despite the widespread "I already know everything" attitude, there are still bikers out there who want to learn. Learning at the mountain bike school begins with the basics: adjusting the

seat, using the gears, not squeezing the front brake alone, stuff like that. Next, it's preride stretches, then an easy cruise over gentle terrain. Once all that's behind you—after about an hour and a half—the fun begins.

You start with climbing a steep side hill that leans just enough to the left to toss unwary bikers into the puckerbrush. Then you move onto a deeply rutted dirt path and learn to spin while avoiding slick rocks and even slicker roots. Once that's done, you swoop down a grassy ski slope crossed by 2-foot-high hummocks every 40 feet. Next, you work on log hopping, starting with a single branch and working up to three stacked tree trunks. There's also expert instruction in single-track steering; ascending and descending very steep terrain; and mastering the more difficult technical moves.

By the end of the session, you're able to take your bike just about anywhere without dismounting. As a bonus, four-day students learn to fix flats, adjust chains, and take their bikes apart and put them back together.

At Mount Snow, you can either bring your own wheels or use one of their late-model bikes at no extra charge. All you need is a sturdy pair of shoes, a reasonably able body, and the willingness to learn.

•FAQ• **I just discovered that on my last ride, I had the front ring on high and the back gear on low. Everybody tells me this will ruin the chain. How badly have I damaged it?**
According to repair expert David Porter, unless you rode hundreds, maybe thousands of miles, you haven't damaged it. "Damage is a gradual process when using these crossover gears, and it occurs on the chain ring and to a lesser extent the cog in the back. In both places, it's more like accelerated wear than discernible damage." ■

RESOURCES

What follows is but a sampling of what's out there that's of interest to backcountry bikers: books, magazines, videos, and websites. Remember, it's only a sample, but if you let one reference lead to another, you'll soon be immersed in the world of backroad and offroad biking.

BOOKS

Bicycling Magazine's 250 Best Cycling Tips, Rodale Press, 1998
> A handy little, forty-eight-page book filled with short tips—some useful, some obvious.

John Barnett, *Barnett's Manual,* 3rd ed., Velo Press, 1996
> A detailed guide to building bicycle wheels and more for the serious home mechanic. One thing, though: It costs $130.

Jobst Brandt, *The Bicycle Wheel,* Avocet, 1993
> Everything anyone ever wanted to know about bike wheels. A classic.

Kate Carter, *Vermont: A Guide to the Classic Trails,* Menasha Ridge Press, Birmingham, AL, 1998
> Because there are so many regional bike guides, I purposely haven't listed them here; they're available from local bookstores and bike shops. But I made one exception. Kate Carter's book is a model for other books. It's written with a light touch, is charmingly photographed, and provides history and eccentricity along with mileage and vertical rise.

Nicky Cowther, *The Ultimate Mountain Bike Book,* Motorbooks, Osceola, WI, 1997
> Since this is essentially a beginner's book, the *"Ultimate"* may be a bit misleading, but it covers a broad range of mountain bike topics.

John Forester, *Bicycle Transportation*, 2nd ed., MIT Press, 1994
> If you want to dive deep into bicycling theory and practice, this book and *Effective Cycling*, by the same author, are good launch sites. I know of no more thoughtful (or opinionated) author on cycling than Forester.

John Forester, *Effective Cycling*, 6th ed., MIT Press, Cambridge, MA, 1993
> Of his controversial argument that cyclists are better off in traffic than on recreation paths, Forester says, "Heavy traffic is not one of the joys of life, but once you learn how to ride in traffic you will realize that you are a partner in a well-ordered dance."

Dan Hope, *Mountain Biking*, Meredith, 1995
> A nicely produced, clearly written guide to the mountain bike. It includes some travel, some maintenance, some history.

Howard Sutherland, *Sutherland's Handbook for Bicycle Mechanics*, 6th ed., Sutherland Publications, 1995
> This $140 plus, Manhattan-phonebook-size book is not for the mechanically faint of heart. It's filled with well-organized tables of what's interchangeable or compatible and what isn't. More than forty-five thousand copies have been sold since the first edition was published in 1974.

Willie Weir, *Spokesongs*, Pineleaf Productions, Seattle, 1997
> Sweet vignettes of a two-wheeled journey through life, with emphasis on India, South Africa, and the Balkans. Many of them were originally broadcast on public radio station KUOW in Seattle.

Lennard Zinn, *Mountain Bike Owner's Manual*, Velo Press, 1998
> A handy pocket-size manual that you can whip out for quick repair advice when you run into trouble deep in the woods.

Lennard Zinn, *Zinn and the Art of Mountain Bike Maintenance*, 2nd edition, Velo Press, 1997
> Great line drawings, clear language, superb organization. If you're repairing a mountain bike or any bike, get this book.

MAGAZINES

Adventure Cyclist
> Free to members of Adventure Cycling Association, *Adventure Cyclist* is about the most useful bike mag I've come across. Useful, readable tips on gear, nutrition, and technique mixed with trip essays on the cycling life. They're on the Internet at website http:www.adv-cycling.org.

Bicycle USA
    Six issues per year of *Bicycle USA* magazine keep League of American Bicyclists members in touch with league activities. Regular features include effective cycling tips, columns, cycle news, and an event calendar. For more information on the league, call (202) 822-1333.

Bicycling Magazine
    It bills itself as "the world's largest cycling publication." Recent articles include "Ten Dumb Ways to Crash," "Armstrong: The Latest Wheaties Champion," and "Five Comfort-Boosting Habits."

Bicyclist
    A general-interest cycling magazine with good gear reviews, exotic travel stories, racing news, and health tips.

bike
    Well written articles, exciting photos, sometimes overly hip—a good step toward mountain bike dude-ism.

Cycle California!
    While its focus is on California biking, this newsprint magazine has articles of interest to cyclists everywhere. For example, it nicely compares club events in New Zealand (friendly, encouraging, cooperative) with those back home (aloof, disparaging, competitive) and helps you plan a solo cycle trip from Oregon through California. The magazine is free.

Cycling USA
    For members of the U.S. Cycling Federation; mostly about racing.

Dirt Rag
    Now this is a strange little magazine. Consider the publisher's note: "WARNING: Magazine reading is an exciting but dangerous pastime; please read the operating procedure on page 126 before opening this magazine. The publisher and his or her heirs will not be held liable if such calamities as eyestrain or paper cuts occur during the operation of the publication." Or this bit of prose from their columnist, the Old Coot: "One thing all ov us has in common is a need fer tires. Cause without em, none ov us could ride our bikes." The magazine, which is as organized as a dog's breakfast, does contain useful information, including the best description I've seen of how suspension systems work and what disorders women can incur from too much time in the saddle.

Mountain Bike
> A general-interest mountain bike magazine that's been around a long time, probably because it covers the waterfront. Whatever your level of experience and expertise, sooner or later you'll find an article that you can't put down.

Mountain Bike Action
> We used to write and shoot for these guys, and oh, how I loved it! Whenever I'd say which magazine the picture was for, a dude-in-training would leap forward to volunteer to flip over his handlebars and into that 2-foot-deep puddle of mud. MBA is the *National Enquirer* of mountain bike mags.

Pedal
> A mixed bag from Canada. Good, honest reviews; cross-Canada cycling news; breathy articles heavy on exclamation marks.

Pro Bike News
> Newsletter of the Bicycle Federation of America. Little about cycles; lots about federal highway legislation. Very interesting stuff for those concerned about making the world a more bike-friendly place.

Tandem Magazine
> A quarterly that features tandem road tests, product reviews, travel stories, rally coverage, a calendar of events, and more. It is the only publication of its kind in the world.

Total Mountain Bike
> Next time you're in Great Britain, pick up a copy. Besides the usual reviews, rides, and races, they give away a lot of bikes.

VeloNews
> Although it's a magazine for racers, nearly every issue contains useful tips for repairing bikes and improving cycling skills.

VIDEOS

Cycling: Repair, Correct Riding Position, Safety, Bosworth/Graves Visual Communications
> Master technician Ron Sulphin walks you through more advanced repairs and preventive maintenance, projects like rebuilding a freewheel, which require specialized tools and great patience. It is my journalistic responsibility to report that the combination of Sulphin's sonorous voice, static camera work, and a multitude of tiny parts put my photographer to sleep in three minutes and forty-two seconds.

Last Ride and/or The Great Vermont Bicycle Toss, Edwards Films
"Once a year, deep in the Vermont woods, bicycle mechanics gather to vent their frustrations on the chain-store bicycle, which stubbornly resists repair." The video shows the pagan rites of tossing, smashing, and trashing these unfortunate bikes. Points are awarded for how far a bike is tossed and how many parts are broken on impact.

Ned Overend's Performance Mountain Biking, Performance Video
Mountain bike legend Ned Overend demonstrates and coaches you through steep descents, hairy climbs, sucking mud, and much more. Best line: "Sand is evil." Blessedly free of punk bravado and ear-splitting soundtrack.

Surviving the Trail, Tumbleweed Films
How to fix a flat, repair a chain, true a wheel, adjust a brake, and more repair techniques. Nice country fiddle music and one hell of a rider. I like that they have women making all the repairs.

Tread, Oak Creek Films
All that's right and all that's wrong with mountain biking in a single film. Two dudes roam around climbing mountains, leaping off cliffs, doing tricks that defy both gravity and explanation. The dudes, Hans Rey and Greg Herbold, can do things on two wheels that most of us can only dream of. But the film, which is sponsored by half the major players in mountain biking, is aimed at attracting overadrenalized male youth to a sport that should be marketing itself to families, commuters, weekend pleasure seekers, and other mere mortals. While the industry furrows its collective brow over why more people aren't taking up the sport, it ought to take a hard look at its promotional focus.

WEBSITES
www.bikecrawler.com
This is a link to all sorts of bike-related websites, from manufacturers to overseas vacations.

www.Bikelane.com
A great source of cycling info of all kinds. Bike companies, teams, races, tips, tours, websites—all there for your browsing pleasure.

www.cyclery.com
Another cyber center for cyclists seeking information on the Internet. Includes 250 electronic mailing lists, all for the bicyclist.

www.gearhead.com
    Like others, this on-line magazine combines chats, reviews, news, and
    more. It's for road and mountain bikers, newbies, and gearheads.
www.mtbr.com
    Buy and sell, product reviews, trail reviews, chatrooms, even an auc-
    tion house, all on-line. Being reader-driven, it gets pretty frank.
www.mtbinfo.com
    Mountain Bike Information Service
    A general store and hometown paper for dirt bikers. Trail guides, bike
    doctor, classifieds, buying advice.
www.usacycling.org
    Official site of the National Off-Road Bicycle Association (NORBA). It
    has everything you need to know about racing, including time and
    place of upcoming events, registration forms, and tips from experts.
http://extreme.nas.net
    Not just for extremists, the Extreme Mountain Biking site has articles,
    tips, reviews, and a buy-and-sell column, plus links to other mountain
    bike sites.
www.trailmonkey.com
    Want to find a hiking and biking trail? Name the place. The trail mon-
    key will show you the trail and give you hints on food to pack, drinks
    to mix, and breweries to tour.
www.cyberportal.net/jwarren/seth/tires
    Buggy's Mountain Bike Tire home page. Everything you always
    wanted to know about tires, plus links to manufacturers' pages.
http://world.std.com/~jimf/biking/slang.html
    A dictionary of mountain bike slang.
http://homepages.together.net/~tara/index.htm
    The Ultimate Mountain Biking home page. Filled with links to bike
    and bike product companies, plus racing schedules and commentaries.
www.imba.com
    International Mountain Bicycling Association (IMBA) site. The voice
    of responsible off-road biking around the world.

INDEX

Page numbers in italics refer to photo captions.

A

Accessories and clothing
  bells, 37
  gloves, padded, 15, 40
  helmets, 41, 43, *50*, 51, 66, 137
  hydration systems, backpack, 41, *43*
  lights, 37
  mirrors, 35–36, *36*
  racks, 37–38, *38*, *39*
  reflectors, 37
  seatpost spring, 43–44
  shorts, padded, 39–40
  sunglasses, 40
  water bottle/cage system, 40–41, 143
  for winter riding, 103, 105–6, *105*
Adventure Cycling Association, 99
Adventure Cyclist, 43
AK-32 Advanced Mechanic Tool Kit, 113
Arm Skins, 103, *105*

B

Back pain, lower-, 150
Balsams Grand Resort Hotel (N.H.), 17,
  44–45, *45*
Bar ends, 17, *18*
Bayley-Hazen Military Road (Vt.), 53, 55
Bells, 37
Bicycling, 100, 138, 139
Bike and equipment, buying
  brakes, 15–16, 32
  collapsible bikes, 31
  cost, 5, 25, 27–28
  fitting, 25, 27–28, *29*, 30
  frame, 12–13, 25, 27
  future trends, 31–33
  gears, 32
  handlebars, 16–17, *17*, *18*
  hubs, 32
  kickstand, 16
  mail-order bikes, 30–31
  mountain bike vs. hybrid, 8, *9*, 10–12, *11*
  pedals, 22, *22*, *23*, 24
  saddles, 18–20, *19*, *20*, 138–39, *140*, 151
  shifters, 13–14, *13*, *14*
  suspension systems, 7, 14–15, *14*, *15*, 32–33
  tires/tubes, 20–21
  try before you buy, 5, 7
  types of mountain bikes, 7
  weight, 5, 25, *25*, 27
  where to buy, 27–28, 30–31
Bike Friday collapsible bike, 31
BK-2 Roll-Up Workshop, 113–14, *113*
Blais, Jean-Marc, 140
Blende, Sonny, 141–44
Books, list of, 161–62
Bottom bracket tool, *113*, 119
Brakes, 15–16, 32
  adjusting, 127, 129, *129*
Braking, 48, 67, 69
  downhill, 74, 76, 78–79, *78*
Breeze, Joe, 43
Brodie Bikes, 67
Bursitis, trochanteric, 150
Burwell, David, 99

C

Cable and housing cutter, *113*, 114, *114*
Cadence, 48, 52
Camelbak hydration system, 41
Campagnolo gearing system, 32
Carpal tunnel syndrome, 150
Carter, Kate, 27–28, *27*, 152
Chain maintenance/repair, 115, *117*,
  118, *126*, *129*
Chainring maintenance/repair, 115, *115*,
  116, *126*
Chain tool, *113*, 114, 115, *117*
Chain whip, *113*, 114, 115, *115*
Cleaner/degreaser, 127, *127*
Clothing. *See* Accessories and clothing
Clubs, 101
Collapsible bikes, 31
Columbia bikes, 5
Competitions and races, 153–54, *154*,
  155, 156–59, *156*
Cone wrench, 114, 120, *120*
Confederation Trail (P.E.I.), 2–3
Craftsbury Outdoor Center (Vt.), 141, 154,
  156–57
Crank wrench and puller, *113*, 114, 118, *119*
Cross-country bikes, 7
Cross-training alternatives, 144–46

D

Danford, Greg, 72, 76, 79
Deer, 59–60

DeFeet, 103
Derailleur adjustments, 129–30, *130, 132*
Diet. *See* Nutrition
Dogs, 59
Downhill bikes, 7
Drafting, 49–51, *49*
Drop-offs, 83–84, *84*

E
Ellis, Wanda, 62

F
Falling, 87–88, *87, 88*
Fascitis, plantar, 152
Family biking, *97*
    clubs, 101
    finding the perfect ride, 97–98
    Le Tour de la Montagne Bromont, 91, 93
    long-distance vacation, 94–97
    tandem riding, 93–94
    tours, 91, 93, 100, 101
    where to go, 99–100
Fennell, Lary, 140
Fitness
    cross-training alternatives, 144–46
    getting fit, 139–41
    injuries, 146–47, 149–52
    sexual problems, preventing, 138–39, *140*
Foot numbness (parasthesias), 151
Formula brakes, 32
Frame
    materials, 12–13
    size, 25, 27
Franconia Notch Bicycle Path (N.H.), 53
Free-ride bikes, 7
Full-suspension (softtail) bikes, 7, 15
Fundy Trail Parkway (N.B.), 62

G
Gear brush, *113,* 114, 115, *116, 117*
Gears, 32
Gloves, padded, 15, 40
Goldstein, Dr. Irwin, 138, 139
Green Gear Cycling, 31
Greenway Alliance, 99
Grip Shift shifters, 13–14, *13*
Grouse Mountain (Vancouver, B.C.), 90

H
Handlebars, 16–17, *17, 18*
    bar ends for, 17, *18*
Hardtail bikes, 7, 15
Hayes brakes, 32
Headset wrench, 122, 124
Helmets, 41, 43, *50,* 51, 66, 137
Herrick, Andrew, 132, 135
Hewitt, Ben, 93–94
Hex wrench, *113,* 114, 125
Hills
    climbing, 52, 72–73, *73, 74*
    descending, 74, 76, *77,* 78–79, *78,* 83–84, *84*

Hite Rite seatpost spring, 43–44
Horses, 58–59
Hubs, 32
Hybrid vs. mountain bike, 8, *9,* 10–12, *11*
Hydra Extreme hydration system, 41
Hydration systems, backpack, 41, *43*

I
Iliotibial band syndrome, 149
IMBA (International Mountain Bicycling
    Association) rules of the trail, 70
Injuries
    back pain, lower-, 150
    bursitis, trochanteric, 150
    carpal tunnel syndrome, 150
    fascitis, plantar, 152
    foot numbness (parasthesias), 151
    iliotibial band syndrome, 149
    knee, biker's (patellofemoral pain
        syndrome), 151
    neck pain, 149–50
    neuropathy, ulnar, 150
    preventing, 146–47, 152
    saddle problems, 138–39, *140,* 151
    tendinitis, 151, 152
    treating, 147–52

J
Jay Peak (Vt.), 55, *55*

K
Kennett, Paul, 146, 158
Kettle Valley Rail-Trail (B.C.), 99
Kickstand, 16
Kita, Joe, 138
Knee, biker's (patellofemoral pain
    syndrome), 151

L
La Route Verte (Montreal, Que.), 100
League of American Bicyclists, 47
Le Tour de la Montagne Bromont, 91, 93
Le tour de l'Île, 100
Lights, 37
Lockring tool, *113,* 114, 115, *116*
Loon Mountain (N.H.), 53
Lubes, 127, *127,* 132, 135

M
Magazines, list of, 162–64
Mail-order bikes, 30–31
Maintenance and repairs, 110, *113. See
    also* Tools
    backroad, 125, *126, 127, 127,* 129–30, *129,
        130, 132, 132,* 135, *135*
    brake adjustments, 127, 129, *129*
    chain, 115, *117, 118, 126, 129*
    chainring, 115, *115, 116, 126*
    cleaner/degreaser, 127, *127*
    derailleur adjustments, 129–30, *130, 132*
    flats, fixing, *113,* 114, 120, *121,* 122, *122, 123*

home, 113–15, *113, 114, 115, 116, 117,* 118,
    118, 119, 120 *120, 121,* 122 *122, 123,*
    124–25, *124*
lubes, 127, *127,* 132, 135
tire/tube pressure, 1–2
washing, 109–10, *109*
wheel emergency repair, 132, *135*
Mavic electronic shifting system, 32
Micro tool Boxes, 113
Mirrors, 35–36, *36*
Montreal (Que.), 100
Moose, 59
Mountain Bike Vermont (Carter), 27, *27*
Mountain bike vs. hybrid, 8, *9,* 10–12, *11*
Mountain biking, overview of, 1
Mount Snow (Vt.), 159–60
Mud, 81, 83, *83*
Mustache handlebars, 17

N
Neck pain, 149–50
Nesbitt, David, 17, 28, 30, 44, 76
Neuropathy, ulnar, 150
New England Mountain Bike Festival, 11
Nitto handlebars, 17
NORBA (National Off-Road Bicycle
    Association), 158
Nutrition. *See also* Water
    basic guidelines, 141–42, 144
    long ride, during a, 143
    preride meal, 142–43
    recovery, 143–44
    tips, 48
    training diets, 142

O
Obstacles, 79, *79, 80,* 81, *81*
Occleshaw, Steve, 146–47
Overend, Ned, 69, 71, 72–73, 76, 78

P
Padley, Greg, 7, 31–33
Palm Beach (Fla.), 33–34
Parasthesias (foot numbness), 151
Park Tool usa, 113
Patellofemoral pain syndrome
    (biker's knee), 151
PCS-1 Home Mechanic Repair Stand, 113
Pedaling, 67
Pedals, 22, *22, 23,* 24
Pedal wrench, 124–25, *124*
Pedro's USA, 132
    Extra Dry, 135
    Ice Wax, 125
    Synlube ATB, 135
    Synlube ROAD, 135
Platypus water reservoir, 41
Porter, David, 19, 24, 31, 76, 88, 160
Presta valves vs. Schraeder valves, 21
Prince Edward Island, 2–3, 100
Pump, 36–37, *123,* 125

Q
Quest hydration systems, 41

R
Racks
    rear-end, 38, *39*
    top-loading, 37–38, *38*
Rails-to-Trails Conservancy, 99
Rails-to-Trails movement, 2, 99
Rainy days and wet roads, 137–38
Rapid-Fire shifters, 13–14, *14*
Reed, Larry, 103, 105–6
Reflectors, 37
Repairs. *See* Maintenance and repairs
Repair stand, 113, *113*
Repetitive Strain Injury (RSI), 14
Riding techniques/tips
    braking, 48, 67, 69, 74, 76, 78–79, *78*
    cadence, 48, 52
    deer, 59–60
    on dirt roads, 57–60, *58*
    dogs, 59
    drafting, 49–51, *49*
    drop-offs, 83–84, *84*
    falling, 87–88, *87, 88*
    hills, climbing, 52, 72–73, *73, 74*
    hills, descending, 74, 76, *77,* 78–79, *78,*
        83–84, *84*
    horses, 58–59
    IMBA rules of the trail, 70
    moose, 59
    mud, 81, 83, *83*
    obstacles, 79, *79,* 80, 81, *81*
    offroad, 65–67, 69–74, *69, 71, 73, 74,* 76,
        77, 78–79, *78, 79, 80,* 81, *81,* 83–84, *83,*
        84, 86, 87–88, *87, 88*
    on paved roads, 47–52, *48*
    pedaling, 67
    sand, 83
    shifting, 48–49, 51–52, 60, 72, 88, 106,
        140, 160
    tricks, 84, *84, 86,* 87
    turning, 69, 71–72, *71*
    for winter riding, 103, 105–6
Rigid bikes, 7
Rivendale catalog, 17

S
Sachs and Rohloff hubs, 32
Sachs P-C chain, 115
Saddles, 18–20, *19, 20*
    problems, 138–39, *140,* 151
Safety
    falling, 87–88, *87, 88*
    general tips, 137
    helmets, 41, 43, *50,* 51, 66, 137
    injuries, 146–47, 149–52
    rainy days and wet roads, 137–38
    winter riding, 103, 105–6, *105*
Sand, 83
S&S collapsible bikes, 31

Scholz, Alan, 31
Scholz, Hans, 31
Schools, 159–60
Schraeder valves vs. Presta valves, 21
Schubert, John, 43–44, 47–48, 71–72, 141
Schwinn bikes, 5, 22
Seawall bike path, 89–90
Sexual problems, preventing, 138–39, *140*
Shifters, 13–14, *13, 14*
Shifting, 60
    choosing the right gear, 51–52, 88, 106,
        140, 160
    hill climbing and, 48–49, 72–73
Shimano
    cartridge tool, 114, 118
    drive systems, 115
    hubs, 32
    Hyperglide (HP) chain, 115
    Interglide (IP) chain, 115
    Mega-9 gearing system, 32
    Mega-Range gearing system, 32
    shoes, *23*
Shoes, *23*, 24
Shorts, padded, 39–40
SIDI shoes, *23*
Single-speed bikes, 7
Softtail (full-suspension) bikes, 7, 15
Spicer, Bruce, 67, 69
Spinal Tap hydration system, 41
Spokesongs (Weir), 137
Spoke wrench, *113*, 114, 120, *121*
Sunglasses, 40
Suspension systems, 7, 14–15, *14, 15,* 32–33
Sweet, Phil, 30, 147–52

T
Tan, Ezekial, 15
Tandem riding, 93–94
Tendinitis
    achilles, 152
    patellar, 151
Terhune, Jesse, 71, *71,* 79, 158–59
Terry Precision Bicycles for Women, 30
3-in-One oil, 135
Tires/tubes, *7*
    buying, 20–21
    flats, fixing, *113,* 114, 120, *121,* 122, *122, 123*
    inflation range for, 1–2
    levers, 114, 120, *121,* 122
    patch kit, *113,* 114, 122, *122*
Tools. *See also* Maintenance and repairs
    bottom bracket tool, *113, 119*
    cable and housing cutter, *113,* 114, *114*
    chain tool, *113,* 114, 115, *117*
    chain whip, *113,* 114, 115, *115*
    cone wrench, 114, 120, *120*
    crank wrench and puller, *113,* 114, 118, *119*
    gear brush, *113,* 114, 115, *116, 117*
    headset wrench, 122, 124
    hex wrench, *113,* 114, 125
    lockring tool, *113,* 114, 115, *116*
    miscellaneous, 125

pedal wrench, 124–25, *124*
pump, 36–37, *123,* 125
repair stand, 113, *113*
Shimano cartridge tool, 114, 118
spoke wrench, *113,* 114, 120, *121*
tire levers, 114, 120, *121,* 122
tube patch kit, *113,* 114, 122, *122*
Tours, 91, 93, 100, 101
Trans-Canada Trail, 99–100
Tricks, 84, *84, 86,* 87
Turning, 69, 71–72, *71*

V
Vancouver (B.C.), 89–90
Velo-City, 67, 90
Velo Quebec, 100
Vermont Sports Today, 27
Videos, list of, 164–65

W
Water, 65, 66
    bottle/cage system, 40–41, 143
    hydration systems, backpack, 41, *43*
    long ride, during a, 143
WD-40, 135
Websites, list of, 165–66
Weight, bike, 5, 25, *25,* 27
Weir, Willie, 137
Wheel emergency repair, 132, *135*
Where to ride
    Balsams Grand Resort Hotel (N.H.),
        17, 44–45, *45*
    Bayley-Hazen Military Road (Vt.), 53, 55
    Confederation Trail (P.E.I.), 2–3
    Craftsbury Outdoor Center (Vt.), 141, 154,
        156–57
    Franconia Notch Bicycle Path (N.H.), 53
    Fundy Trail Parkway (N.B.), 62
    Grouse Mountain (Vancouver, B.C.), 90
    Jay Peak (Vt.), 55, *55*
    Kettle Valley Rail-Trail (B.C.), 99
    La Route Verte (Montreal, Que.), 100
    Loon Mountain (N.H.), 53
    Mount Snow (Vt.), 159–60
    Palm Beach (Fla.), 33–34
    Rails to Trails movement, 2, 99
    Seawall bike path (Vancouver, B.C.), 89–90
    Trans-Canada Trail, 99–100
Winooski Bike Shop, 19, 24
Winter riding, 103, 105–6, *105*
Wrench
    cone, 114, 120, *120*
    crank, *113,* 114, 118, *119*
    headset, 122, 124
    hex, *113,* 114, 125
    pedal, 124–25, *124*
    spoke, *113,* 114, 120, *121*

Z
Zinn, Lennard, 65–66, 110, 125
Zinn and the Art of Mountain Bike Maintenance
        (Zinn), 110